A Wine Lover's Guide to Virginia Wine

A Taste of Wine series

Edited by

The Wine Professionals Association

D1520519

Contents

Preface..7

Acknowledgments...10

Introduction...11

From Purchase to Pairing...12

   Purchasing 12

   Caring for Wine..13

   Serving..13

   Tasting...15

   Wine Pairing...15

Virginia Wine..17

   Wine is Not Made in Ugly Places...........................17

   Virginia's Climate and Terroir 19

   Support for Virginia Wine 21

American Viticultural Areas of Virginia 24

   Shenandoah Valley AVA...26

   Rocky Knob AVA...28

   North Fork of Roanoke AVA...................................28

   Monticello AVA...29

   Northern Neck George Washington Birthplace AVA..........30

   Virginia's Eastern Shore AVA 30

   Middleburg AVA 31

   Appalachian High Country AVA.............................32

Virginia Peninsula AVA 33

Which Ones Do I Like and Why?.................................34

Central Virginia..34

Northern Virginia 35

The Middleburg AVA 37

Monticello AVA..39

Virginia's Eastern Shore AVA 42

Virginia Peninsula AVA 42

The Shenandoah Valley AVA..43

Southern Virginia 44

Interviews...45

The Scientist...46

The Couple 51

The Godfather of Loudoun Wine...................................56

The Biodynamic Wine Maker...61

Thoughtful Progress 65

The Analyst 77

The Diplomat...84

The Wine Chemist...93

The Oenologist 102

The Historian..113

Virginia's Plantings 123

Tons of Grapes per Year 124

Acres by Grape Type 126

Acres of Hybrid and American Grape Types 127

Virginia Governor's Cup 128

Virginia Governor's Cup Analysis 130

Medals by Virginia Regions 2012-2023 132

Virginia's Trend of Medals 2012-2023 135

Regional Medal Trends 2012-2023 136

Top Three Wineries by Region 137

Governor's Case Analysis 138

Governor's Case by Type and Style 138

Governor's Case Reds vs. Whites 140

Grape Types Used in Governor's Case 141

Governor's Case Grape Origins 2012-2023 143

Regions and Country of Origin of Grapes 144

Loudoun Wine Awards 146

Awards and Medals from 2018-2022 148

Wineries Receiving Awards 149

Best of Class, Gold, Chairman's Grand Awards 150

Grape Types Winning Awards 152

Best of Class, Gold, Chairmans Grand Awards 153

Wine Receiving Awards by Type 155

Award Winning Trends, Red vs. White Wines 156

Award Winning Vintages 156

Findings from good and challenging years...................157

Red Wine Awards by Vintages and Grape Type.............158

White Wine by Vintages and Grape Type....................158

Red vs. White Wine Awards by Vintages 159

Award-winning White grapes in 2018..........................160

Award-Winning Wines in 2019 161

From Harvest Year to Award......................................162

Monticello Cup Wine Competition 163

Awards and Medals by Year 2015-2023 163

Wineries Receiving Awards from 2015-2023 165

Award Winning Single Varietal Wines 166

Award Winning Blends..168

Wine Receiving Awards by Type 169

Award Winning Trends, Red vs. White Wines 170

Award Winning Vintages...171

Red vs. White Wine Awards by Vintages 172

Award-Winning Grapes 2017 172

Shenandoah Cup Wine Competition 173

Medal-Winning Wine Types......................................173

Medal Winning Vintages 174

Medal Winning Wineries 175

Grape Types Winning Medals 176

Virginia State Wine Organizations.............................178

Virginia Vineyards Association 178

The Virginia Wine Board 178

Virginia Winery Distribution Company 179

Virginia Wineries Association 180

Regional Wine Organizations 181

Loudoun Wineries & Winegrowers Association 181

Wine Professionals Association 181

Winemakers Research Exchange 182

The Shenandoah Valley Wine Growers Association 183

Wine Festivals 184

Virginia Wine Expo 184

Taste of Monticello Wine Trail Festival 184

Virginia Wine Festival 184

Shenandoah Valley Wine Festival 185

Helpful wine terms 186

Preface

This book is personal to me. I remember attending a Virginia wine festival at Bull Run State Park in Centreville, Virginia, in the late nineties. I liked most of the wines I tasted, but I was struck by one, an Afton Mountain Riesling. I remember thinking, this is as good as any Riesling I have had. From that point on, I was hooked on Virginia wine.

Virginia is blessed with a vibrant wine industry with many high-quality wine-producing regions. At a minimum, visiting the beautiful wineries while sharing wine with friends and family is a unique pleasure. At best, you know where your wine comes from, you can meet winery owners, and rub shoulders with the winemakers. Supporting local wineries is rewarding, and it contributes to the fabric of a community, creates jobs, preserves land, and ensures a way of life for generations to come.

One must realize where Virginia is now, remembering that it was not until 1976 that wine production was restarted in Virginia post-prohibition. The world's great wine regions have been sifting and sorting grape varieties for centuries to match their growing conditions. They gained experience caring for vineyards, blending their wines, and creating wine styles that satisfy market demands and pair with local cuisine. It takes time!

I have become an advocate for Virginia wine while experiencing the growth in wineries and the quality improvement as vintages pass. It is common for Virginia wines to win medals in out-of-state competitions, be lauded in notable magazines, and be rated highly by wine critics. I visit local wineries near home in Loudoun County, Virginia, further south to the Monticello AVA and throughout the state at every opportunity. On weekends our family and friends take day trips to wineries, and when out-of-towners visit, I insist on taking them to Virginia wine country.

The path to publishing this book has been challenging and enjoyable. In 2019, after studying for a year, I passed the Certified Specialist of Wine (CSW) exam the Society of Wine Educators offers. I immediately wanted to write books but was advised first to research, write, and publish articles, which I did for eighteen months on my website *worldofvino.com* and still do. All the while, I was building up a small following on social media and studying for the next level of wine certification. I also experienced all the wine I reasonably could at social events, wine vacations, private wine tastings, and at home.

The time finally came for writing books, and morning after morning; my ritual was to wake before sunrise, research, analyze, and write for hours each day. My first books are available in paperback, hardcover, and Kindle format on Amazon; they are part of my *A Taste of Wine* series, as is this book. The first book is *A Wine Lover's Guide to European Wine*, and the second is *A Wine Lover's Guide to New World Wine*. I departed from a broad scope in my third book and focused on pairing food with October One Vineyard's wine. I sincerely hope you are helped, guided, informed, and inspired by these works.

Acknowledgments

Many thanks to all those in the world of wine that had gone before and laid solid ground for others to tread. I could not have written this book without these wonderful works: Karen MacNeil's The Wine Bible, Madeline Puckette and Justin Hammack's The Essential Guide to Wine, David Bird's Understanding Wine Technology, the Society of Wine Educators CSW Study Guide, and The Oxford Companion to Wine. I also want to thank my mother, who taught me to smell everything. My father taught me to be quiet, listen, and think. My children never stop teaching me things, and my wife teaches me patience. I am very grateful to the people that granted me interviews. Of all the activities associated with writing this book, my time listening and learning from them was the most rewarding.

Introduction

This is a book of samples. When testing the purity of a large and dynamic body of water, it is unnecessary to test all the water it contains. It only requires collecting and analyzing water samples from critical locations to determine the answer.

Likewise, it is unnecessary to evaluate all of Virginia's grape types, interview all its winemakers, taste all its wine, or know all of Virginia's wine organizations to gain an understanding and appreciation of Virginia's wine.

I have organized a sample of data from reliable sources so that the curious wine lover knows Virginia's wine in a way not possible before.

I demonstrate the location and amount of the wine grapes Virginia uses, analyze four key wine competition results, interview a sample of wine personalities, taste their wine, and bring to light critical wine-related organizations in Virginia.

The popular one-hundred-point rating system on some wine labels was made famous by wine expert Robert Parker. Knowing an expert's ratings can help; remember that not all wine is rated, and there is no substitute for tasting for yourself. The 100-point rating system considers the clarity, depth of color, aroma intensity, sweetness, acidity, bitterness, tannin, alcohol, body, flavors, complexity, and finish. The rating is relative to other wines of that type; for example, a 92-point California Chardonnay is a rating among Chardonnays from that region.

Wine rating scores used by a significant wine reviewing firm:

60-69 flawed and not recommended.

70-79 deficient and taste average.

80-84 above average to good.

85-90 good to very good.

90-94 superior to exceptional.

12

95-100 benchmark examples or classics.

Wine-reviewing companies with online and subscription-based information are plentiful; three well-known entities are Wine Spectator (WS), The Wine Advocate (WA), and Wine Enthusiast (WE). You may see their ratings included with wine descriptions in wine stores.

Caring for Wine

In the short term, after purchasing wine, keep it cool and out of sunlight; for long-term cellaring, attempt to replicate the conditions of a cave. Keep the temperature stable between 50-59 degrees Fahrenheit, the humidity at 60-75%, and eliminate light exposure.

Serving

The usual alcohol range for wine is 12% to 15% average alcohol by volume (ABV), with 12% as the average. For comparison, beer is 5% ABV, and liquor is 40% ABV on average. Aerate red wine in a decanter, a bowl, or glasses at least fifteen minutes before serving, longer for complex wines. Aerating or allowing the wine to breathe mixes oxygen with the wine improving the aromas and flavors. Just removing the cork alone will not expose the wine to enough oxygen. Decanting old wine leaves sediment behind; it can be bitter and unsightly. Use good quality wine glasses with a thin rim to concentrate the aromas to your nose. Serve wine at a proper temperature to improve the aroma and flavor. After opening a bottle, keep the temperature stable with ice for sparkling and sweet wine and a ceramic wine sleeve for all others. For maximum enjoyment, follow these temperature guidelines.

Sweet white 43°F - 47°F

Sparkling 43°F - 50°F

Light whites and rosés 45°F - 50°F

Medium to full-bodied dry white 50°F - 55°F

Light-bodied reds 50°F - 55°F

Medium-bodied reds 55°F

Full-bodied and aged reds 59°F - 64°F

Refrigerator temperature is between 37°F - 40°F.

Room temp. 72°F; neither is optimal for serving wine.

Knowing the components of wine and how they affect your tasting experience is essential. Dry wines have no detectable sweetness, off-dry or semi-sweet wines have a little sweetness, sweet wines are noticeably sweet, and dessert wines are thick with sweetness.

Wine's acidity will cause you to pucker, as when eating a tart apple, tannins will dry your mouth, alcohol may cause your nose or throat to burn somewhat, and bitterness is detected at the back of your tongue and may be caused by tannins. After swallowing, look for a pleasant finish, a lingering taste; the longer, the better.

Also, look for odd, off, or unbalanced tastes or if the wine's flavor does not linger. These are signs of low-quality, flawed, or poorly made wines.

Wine Pairing

Wine should complement or intensify food components; for example, acidic Chianti amplifies acidic tomato sauce, and an acidic unoaked Chardonnay complements creamy cheeses. The shared components of food and wine are sweetness, acidity, bitterness, savoriness, power, and intensity. The wine should be sweeter when serving something sweet than the food item. When pairing wine, consider the salt, fat, strength of flavors, serving temps, and food preparation type. Try out pairings before serving them to guests; there is no substitute for food and wine pairing experimentation.

Virginia Wine

Virginia ranks fifth in wine production in the U.S., with eight AVAs producing delicious wine from many European grapes, but primarily French grapes, French-American hybrids, and the indigenous Norton grape. East Coast winegrowers face more difficult vineyard conditions than California growers, with high summer humidity that fosters mold and disease followed by cold winters that can harm vines. However, with careful planning and investigation, growers have found soil, sun, and a climate suitable for producing beautiful wines.

Expect neither a French nor California-style wine from Virginia; its style is less fruity than California wines and not as earthy and minerally as French wines. Virginia red wines are restrained and savory with medium acidity and smooth tannins. The best ones are well structured, improve with age, and are great food wines. Virginia uses American oak, French oak, and Acacia wood barrels for aging in many of its wines.

Wine is Not Made in Ugly Places

Queen Elizabeth I of England, the virgin queen, was beautiful, and so is the countryside of her namesake Virginia,

USA, from the Shenandoah Valley to the Blue Ridge Mountains to the rolling hills of the Piedmont to the Coastal Plain, the Chesapeake Bay shores, and on to the Atlantic. It is just beautiful. Virginia's wine country has charming small towns that welcome thirsty weekenders on wine getaways.

Wineries are located across the state, but the majority are clustered in high concentrations in the eastern foothills of the Blue Ridge Mountains starting from Northern Virginia and extending southwest to Charlottesville and beyond. One interesting note is that in Charlottesville, Jefferson Vineyards in the Monticello AVA produces award-winning wine on a portion of Thomas Jefferson's estate.

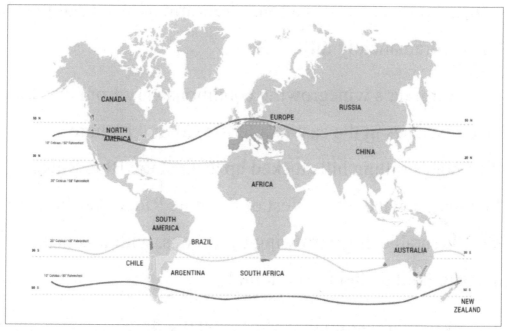

Virginia is well within the world's temperate-wine-producing zone.

Virginia is well within the world's temperate-wine-producing zones, 30-50 degrees above and below the equator. It falls on the same latitudes as California's more northern wine areas of the North Coast AVA down to the top of the Central Coast AVA. It is interesting to note that on the same latitudes traveling east across the Atlantic are renowned wine-growing regions: south-central Portugal, southern Spain, Sicily, the tip of the boot of Italy, and Greece.

Most of Virginia's climate is humid sub-tropical under the Köppen climate classification. The warm, moist air of the Gulf Stream dramatically influences it.

Virginia's winegrowing conditions vary from maritime sandy beaches in the east to a fertile Coastal Plain to Piedmont's rolling hills tucked up against the Blue Ridge Mountains in the west. West of the Blue Ridge has the state's most favorable grape growing conditions, with less than average rainfall and lower humidity.

Virginia's geology is exceptionally diverse, consisting of five major geologic regions ranging from 5,700 plus feet elevation in the west to sea level in the east. Sandstone and limestone pervade the soil west of the Blue Ridge Mountains, including the Shenandoah River Valley. The Blue Ridge Mountains and Piedmont consist of metamorphic rock and volcanic soils. Sandstone and shale dominate the Blue Ridge, while gneiss, schist, and greenstone make up the Piedmont. The Coastal Plain is comprised of sand and clay as it slopes toward the sea in Virginia's eastern parts.

In support of the Virginia wine industry, the State of Virginia created the nonprofit Virginia Winery Distribution Company (VWDC) that assists distribution to local retailers, thus helping consumers access wine and businesses by reducing distribution costs.

Colleges & universities support the Virginia wine industry; a couple of examples are the Northern Virginia Community College (NVCC) has offered Viticulture and Oenology classes started by collaboration between the Virginia wine industry, the state, and academia. The purpose is to supply the Virginia wine industry with educated staff and foster industry growth.

Virginia Tech. College of Agriculture and Life Sciences offers a minor in Viticulture for students interested in grape production and winemaking. It provides an interdisciplinary learning experience in wine grape production, wine-making, and wine business and marketing.

Also, the Department of Food Science and Technology at Virginia Tech has a long history of providing an Enology

Extension to serve the needs of the Commonwealth of Virginia. The enology extension program offers services and programs to new and existing wineries. Graduate students in the department also can conduct research focused on fermentation-related issues, including winemaking, beer brewing, and fermented foods that provide additional resources for Virginia wineries. In addition, the Analytical Services Laboratory has served the Virginia wine and fermented beverage industries since 2006 with full-service and custom analysis on wine, beer, distilled spirits, cider, juice, kombucha, and food products.

Virginia Polytechnic Institute and State University's Alson H. Smith Jr. Agricultural & Research Extension Center help commercial grape growers by providing workshops, courses, on-site consulting, technical material, training, and problem resolution. In addition, growers benefit greatly from Virginia Polytechnic Institute and State University's Alson H. Smith Agricultural Center in Winchester for invaluable research.

Most importantly, the public supports the Virginia wine industry with their dollars. The Economic Impact Study of Wine & Wine Grapes on the Commonwealth of Virginia-2015 shows that the number of people visiting Virginia wineries grew from 1.6 to 2.25 million between 2010 and 2015.

Now the Virginia wine industry generates $1.37 billion in economic impact to the state annually and, as of 2019, employs over eight-thousand people. I love the attitude and determination of Jack Kent Cook and their Family, owners of Boxwood Estate Winery in Middleburg, Virginia. Boxwood's president John Kent Cook said concerning wine production in Virginia, "I am convinced that Virginia can produce a premium wine as good as anywhere with today's viticultural knowledge and winemaking techniques."

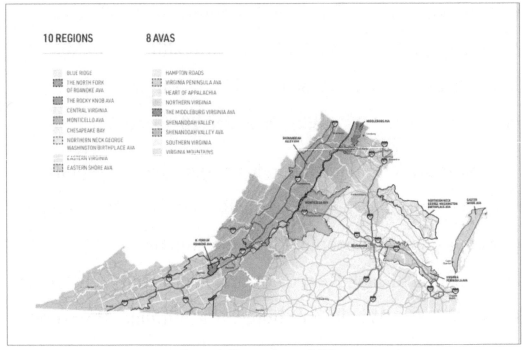

Virginia's Wine regions and AVAs

American Viticultural Areas (AVA) are established by partitioning the federal Alcohol and Tobacco Tax and Trade Bureau (TTB), a bureau under the Department of the Treasury. The TTB defines: "An American Viticultural Area, or AVA, is a specific type of appellation of origin used on wine labels.

An AVA is a delimited grape-growing region with specific geographic or climatic features that distinguish it from the surrounding regions and affect how grapes are grown. Using an AVA designation on a wine label allows vintners to describe the origin of their wines to consumers accurately and helps them identify wines they may purchase".

The Virginia AVAs are Middleburg, Monticello, North Fork of Roanoke, Northern Neck George Washington Birthplace, Rocky Knob, Shenandoah Valley, Virginia's Eastern Shore, and Virginia Peninsula. And the Appalachian High Country AVA, which is shared with neighboring states.

For a wine to include the name of the AVA on its label, at least 85% of the grapes that make up the wine must come from that AVA. Find the TTB's regulations online: *ttb.gov/wine/american-viticultural-area-ava.*

As a matter of course, new AVAs get created out of a need to highlight and market the uniqueness of regions, and it is common to have smaller, more defined AVAs within larger ones. At this point, Virginia is home to eight AVAs located throughout the state, with most of the wine-growing activity occurring in the regions of Central Virginia, Northern Virginia, and the Shenandoah Valley. These regions contain three prominent AVAs of Virginia, the Middleburg AVA in Northern Virginia, the Monticello AVA in Central Virginia, and the Shenandoah Valley AVA west of the Blue Ridge mountains. All three are near and influenced by the Blue Ridge Mountains, a physiographic province of the more extensive Appalachian Mountain Range.

Listed here are the Virginia AVAs in the order they were established over a thirty-nine-year period from nineteen eighty-two up to the present. The most recent AVA was awarded in September of twenty twenty-one.

Shenandoah Valley AVA

Virginia's largest official wine region, the Shenandoah Valley AVA, was the first American Viticultural Area established in Virginia on December 27, 1982. It is in northwestern Virginia and extends into neighboring West Virginia in its northern part. Covering approximately two and a half million acres, it is roughly the size of California's North Coast AVA which covers three million acres and comprises seventeen nested appellations, including the famous Napa Valley AVA.

The Shenandoah Valley AVA is known for its favorable conditions for growing wine grapes. It sits west of the Blue

Ridge Mountains and east of the Allegheny Mountains, shielded from the humidity that blankets most of Virginia and the D.C. region.

The Shenandoah Valley AVA includes the better part of the scenic Shenandoah River, adding to its charm and beauty. The AVA runs through Virginia's Amherst, Augusta, Botetourt, Clark, Frederick, Page, Rockbridge, Rockingham, Shenandoah, and Warren counties. In West Virginia, it is within the counties of Berkeley and Jefferson.

The high elevations, cooler temperatures, a longstanding farming culture, and limited rainfall produce unique, high-quality wines. The Shenandoah Valley's hot days and cool nights are ideal for growing grapes with balanced acidity, fruit sugars, and ripeness, all of which translate into great wine.

Another ingredient contributing to Shenandoah Valley wine is the abundance of limestone, regionally called Bluestone, a beneficial soil component known worldwide for producing great wine. Think of the Chardonnay from Chablis or Pinot Noir from Burgundy; limestone soil is credited for their wine's finesse, acidity, and uniqueness.

Vineyard visits are a breeze in this area due to Interstate #81 running the length of the AVA. Virginia's quaint towns and beauty, mingled with the regional wine, make for unforgettable experiences.

Rocky Knob AVA

The mountainous Rocky Knob AVA, located in Floyd and Patrick counties, was established on January 11, 1983. Notable wineries reside there, such as Chateau Morrisette and Villa Appalachia Winery. Vineyards are located on the eastern slopes of the Blue Ridge Mountains for sun exposure and are planted in well-drained loam and gravel soils. All these components ensure well-structured and intensely flavored wines.

North Fork of Roanoke AVA

The North Fork of Roanoke AVA is located within the Blue Ridge region in southwestern Virginia on the eastern slopes of the Allegheny Mountains within the counties of Montgomery and Roanoke and was established on April 14, 1983. It is a high-elevation AVA with vineyards between 1,200 and 2,200 feet. The AVA is named for its position on the North Fork River before it converges with the South Fork to form the

Roanoke River. It's known for Bordeaux blends and varietal wines made from Cabernet Sauvignon, Cabernet Franc, and Merlot, but winemakers experiment with several other grape varieties.

Monticello AVA

The Monticello AVA produces fine wines with depth of flavor due to excellent vineyard sites, wineries' high expertise, mature vines, and a two-hundred-day growing season. Interestingly, following the 38th parallel from Napa heading east, it cuts straight through the Monticello AVA.

The Monticello AVA is a beautiful area in central Virginia's eastern foothills of the Blue Ridge Mountains. It is fortunate to have the charming town of Charlottesville, Virginia, and the University of Virginia (UVA) at its center. The AVA was established on January 22, 1984, and covers over one thousand square miles in Virginia's central Piedmont, including Albemarle, Fluvanna, Greene, Nelson, and Orange counties.

Monticello's best vineyards are oriented east-southeast at high altitudes for maximum sun exposure. The prominent grapes of this area are Cabernet Franc, Petit Verdot, Chardonnay, Viognier, Sauvignon Blanc, and the indigenous Norton grape. Many of my favorite wineries lie in the Monticello AVA.

Northern Neck George Washington Birthplace AVA

This AVA is within the counties of Westmoreland, King George, Northumberland, Lancaster, and Richmond and was established on April 20, 1987. This AVA is in the Chesapeake Bay area, with the Potomac River forming its northern boundary and the Rappahannock River's southern boundary. These vineyards benefit from the moderating effect of the nearby water. And are home to some of Virginia's most prolific vineyards planted in sandy loam soils. Chardonnay, Cabernet Franc, Vidal Blanc, and Chambourcin do well here.

Virginia's Eastern Shore AVA

Virginia's Eastern Shore AVA was established on January 1, 1991, and is located within the counties of Accomack and Northampton. This AVA is situated on the long narrow Delmarva Peninsula, bordered by the Chesapeake Bay on its west and the Atlantic Ocean on its east. This is a genuinely maritime climate with an extended growing season compared to other AVAs of Virginia. The deep soil of marine deposits, ocean breezes, and the moderating influence of the surrounding water make for bright wines with unique saline characteristics.

Middleburg AVA

The Middleburg AVA is in the foothills of the northern part of the Blue Ridge Mountains. The AVA was established on September 12, 2012, encompassing about two hundred square miles in Loudoun and Fauquier Counties in northern Virginia. Its northern border is the Potomac River, and its southern is Interstate #66. At the center of the AVA is the charming town of Middleburg, with shops, restaurants, and stunning views of the rolling hills, horse farms, and vineyards. The fortunate thing about this wine region is that it is an accessible drive west of the Washington, D.C. metro area, bringing throngs out to wine country for parties, weddings, and weekend getaways.

Many wineries produce Meritage blends with the Bordeaux grapes Cabernet Sauvignon, Merlot, Cabernet Franc, and Petit Verdot. Also, outstanding single-varietal wine is made here using only one grape type: a single-varietal Cabernet Franc is made from 100% Cabernet Franc grapes. The standout whites of this region are Sauvignon Blanc, Viognier, Albariño, and Petit Manseng, which thrive in the Middleburg AVA. The Middleburg AVA has well-placed vineyards, good wine-growing soil, and a cooler climate than its southern neighbors. The Ashby Gap, a break in the Blue Ridge Mountains, brings breezes, moderating fog, and cooling effects from the Shenandoah Valley.

Appalachian High Country AVA

This AVA is located within the Appalachian Mountains and was established on October 26, 2016, and straddles North Carolina, Tennessee, and Virginia. It runs through the North Carolina counties of Alleghany, Ashe, Avery, Mitchell, and Watauga. It is contained in Carter and Johnson counties in Tennessee and Virginia's Grayson County.

The Appalachian High Country AVA has a cool climate, a short growing season, well-drained soil, and high elevations ranging from 1,338 feet to over 6,000 feet. Most vineyards are planted at elevations between 2,290 and 4,630 feet. The high solar irradiance offset the low temperatures and short growing seasons, promoting grape maturation. The terraced vineyards are planted on steep slopes of 30 degrees or greater, requiring hand tending to vineyards. Grape varieties such as Seyval Blanc, Marquette, Marechal Foch, Frontenac, and Vidal Blanc are cold hearty grapes well suited for this cooler high elevation.

Virginia Peninsula AVA

Virginia's newest AVA was established in September of 2021 and is located on the low-elevation coastal plain in James City, York, New Kent, and Charles City counties. It has a maritime climate with deep sedimentary soil and is surrounded by water. The York River makes its northern border, the James River its southern border, and the Chesapeake Bay's western boundary. The long, relatively narrow AVA extends eastward, approximately fifty miles toward Richmond. This AVA has promise as it is situated in a prime tourist region straddling Interstate #64. It is near popular historical sites, tourist attractions, and the main route to beaches from major population centers. Wineries already produce ageable reds with a depth of character, delicate white blends, and single-grape offerings like Viognier.

This is a sample of Virginia wines and is not meant to be an exhaustive list; I have not visited every Virginia winery nor tasted every wine from Virginia. These are some of my favorites based on personal experience.

Central Virginia

Early Mountain Vineyards, Five Forks.

I was in shock in a good way when I tasted this white wine. I immediately turned the bottle around to see the back label, hoping to see a list of what magnificent mix of grapes delivered complexity like this!

I enjoy everything about this wine. The blend of Petit Manseng, Sauvignon Blanc, Malvasia Bianca, and Muscat serves everything my taste buds like.

When tasting wine, I immediately think of what to pair it with. Early Mountain's pairing suggestions say, "Asian fusion menus- tropical & citrus fruit complement the complex heat and rich sauces." And I agree, but this wine is so exceptional, and I would have to devote effort to finding worthy pairings.

Breaux Vineyards, Nebbiolo.

Breaux Vineyards is a welcoming place of sheer beauty and grace. And they make award-winning Nebbiolo! The 2017 Nebbiolo I tasted had a light and fruity attack up front and was packed with red fruit flavors and lots of Nebbiolo energy. A soft cover of sweet flowers and nicely integrated tannins hold this wine together.

Chrysalis Vineyard, Loxley Reserve Norton.

Chrysalis has the world's most extensive indigenous North American Norton grape vineyards. The Loxley Reserve is deep purple-colored and rich, with dark fruit aromas of fresh ripe plum and tart red cherry flavors. This wine has balanced acid and tannic structures and will improve with age.

Hillsborough Vineyards, Tannat.

This is bold, with intense flavors of cherries and something I love on wine, chocolate notes. It is a wine with moderate acidity, nice mincrality, and a touch of vanilla, presumably from barrel aging. A good amount of time aging tames the tannins.

35

Fabbioli Cellars, Tannat.

Fabbioli tames this grape with skill. It is a beautiful deep color, a full-bodied red wine with complex layers of spice. It has the type of red fruit flavors I love, such as cranberry and cherries. It's aged in American oak, which adds depth. The finish is long and satisfying, putting this in my meditation wine category.

Maggie Malick's Wine Cave, Grenache.

This is the only Virginia winery I know of that grows Grenache. Their Grenache blend is leathery, earthy, and pretty; it lures you with wafts of leather, wood, tea, and herbs.

October One Vineyard, Merlot, Albariño.

October One Vineyard makes single-varietal goodness. I like every wine in their lineup. One of my favorites is their 2019 Merlot. It has an appealing, come-get-me aroma with blackberries, bramble, and a touch of spice. With very well-integrated French oak barrel aging, it is deeply colored and sits pretty in the glass. Of all their wines, it is my favorite overall for drinkability, always calling for another glass.

Their Albariño is very popular and a benchmark for this wine in Virginia. This wine has alluring aromatics that call you to taste it. The 2021 has a light body and is a pale golden color that immediately displays beautiful aromas of powdered white flowers and lemon. There are also notes of lemon candy and tropical fruit. The acidity was enough to make my mouth water even before tasting it.

The Middleburg AVA

Boden Young, Albariño.

This is a star of an Albariño, a grape everyone will soon talk about in Virginia. This is a winemaker's wine. It's got it all. It's acidic, balanced, and lively in the glass; the aromas are of tropical fruit with some creamy notes. Also, I get some mango and melon on the nose. I like this wine slightly chilled and with seafood.

Boxwood Estate Winery, Topiary, Reserve.

As a thank-you gift, I once gave a half case of Topiary to a gracious host in Oxford, England. It was available at the Oxford Wine Company, Oxford, England, and was well received by my host.

Topiary is an estate-grown Bordeaux blend. The percentage of grapes varies with each vintage. The last I tried was made from Cabernet Franc, Merlot, and Petit Verdot. This wine has a fruit sweetness, not sugary sweetness; it is light-bodied, has pleasing aromas and tastes, is very balanced, and is a great food wine.

Their Reserve, a Bordeaux-style blend, is one of my all-time favorite red wines from Virginia. They only make this from their best fruit, barrels, and blends in the best years. I get this wine out when we have people over that appreciate wine. It has never disappointed me.

RDV Vineyards, Lost Mountain.

This is an excellent balanced expression of a Bordeaux blend from the Middleburg AVA. This alluring, mouthwatering wine sneaks up on you with tempting oak, spice, and fruit acid at the start. It needs no food, is restrained, supple with blackberry, celery seed, and hints of toffee on the nose.

The medium body drips with richness, and it finishes long. The 2015 I tried was beautiful in the glass; it showed no signs of oxidation and weighed in at a robust 14.5% ABV without giving up a thing.

Ramiiisol Vineyards, Chardonnay, Cabernet Franc.

Their biodynamic wines are beautiful; their Chardonnay is the most expressive I have ever tasted. This wine is pretty and has a bouquet of fresh, delicate powdery flowers smiling at you through a lovely, shimmering medium gold color. Medium weight and a clean mouthfeel with perfectly balanced acidity make it a genuinely delicious wine.

Their Cabernet Franc; instantly taste depth in this wine; it's balanced with low acidity and tannins and is a great food wine. The wine is opaque and deeply colored, with a garnet rim and thin legs. The nose is subtle, with notes of wool, oak, elderberry, veggies, and a hint of vanilla. The grape candy or popsicle flavors are pleasing, calling for another glass.

King Family Vineyards, Viognier, Cabernet Franc, Crosé, Chardonnay.

They have a small-batch series; as part of it, they produce a skin-contact wine, an orange wine, using the Viognier grape.

This wine is an alluring, brick-orange colored wine with lovely weightiness to the wine.

It has an initial supple mouthfeel leading to a cutting edge that keeps my interest, and I can enjoy it without food. I love the aromas of candied fruit, stone fruit, and rich canned peaches or apricots. Its razor-thin tannins and finish call for another sip. Slightly chilled is how I enjoy it best.

King's Cabernet Franc – another member of the small-batch series, is a refreshingly light-bodied Cabernet Franc that prettily dances about in the glass: translucent, subtle fruit sweetness and a somewhat delicate nose. Balanced acid and tannins make it an excellent food wine. I love this as a starter wine accompanying hors d'oeuvres, cheeses, or pâté when white wine will not do. Slightly chilled, it reminds me of a Cru Beaujolais.

Crosé (rosé) is so popular that it creates a stir every year at release time, so line up because this sells out fast and for a good reason. Crosé is an attractive light cranberry-colored rosé that delivers melon and strawberry aromas with a crisp acidic mouthfeel. It has slight bitterness (a good thing) and a sweet floral nose of roses and stone fruit. Serve chilled, a must, with charcuterie, olives, tapenade, crackers, and sharp cheeses.

Their small batch series Chardonnay is the prettiest wine I have ever seen. It just glistens in the glass; it must be captured by an artist if possible.

Michael Shaps Wineworks, Petit Manseng.

This wine is an attractive yellow gold with a nice weight and is smooth and supple on the tongue. The tropical and pleasingly pungent aromas belie the taste and beautiful acidity. I am still determining what I would pair with this, a creamy shrimp dish, perhaps. It never reached that point; when tasting, I just sat and drank my fill; it may be in the Amarone category of meditation wine.

Veritas Vineyards, Viognier

I owe my love for this Northern Rhone grape to Veritas Vineyards and winemaker Emily Hodson. Before my first glass of their 2009 Viognier, I had not experienced white wine with a bouquet that demanded my attention and insisted I taste it. The bright straw color was alluring, the mouthfeel was weighty and almost oily, and the acidity was perfectly balanced. I bought as much of the 2009 vintage as I could. Veritas continues to make excellent Viogniers vintage after vintage.

Chatham Vineyards on Church Creek, Cabernet Franc, Chardonnay.

I let this Cabernet Franc breathe for at least fifteen minutes and tasted it chilled. This is an excellent medium-body food wine with balance, soft tannins, and a beautiful lilting nose with aromas of grape candy, berries, and hints of spice. The 2019 I tasted has an excellent round mouthfeel and a tame alcohol level of 12.5% ABV. I appreciate lower ABV level wine that delivers on taste and structure.

Their steel-fermented Chardonnay, slightly chilled, is a delight that reflects the terroir of the Eastern Shore. It's crisp, with nice acidity, minerality, melon, lemon, and pineapple aromas. And what I call the alluring smell of rain on rocks. And something that is truly a treat, a splash of salt brine on the nose.

Virginia Peninsula AVA

Williamsburg Winery, Adagio.

This is a family favorite, especially for my oldest son and his Polish wife. Every time I go to Poland, I bring Adagio with me, and we have Adagio every time they visit us. Williamsburg Winery has been making this for more than ten years and won award after award.

The Shenandoah Valley AVA

Bluestone Vineyards, Moscato, Chardonnay.

This is one of my favorites from their extensive lineup. This wine has the balance of a surefooted tightrope walker. From the first sip, you are struck with a sweet delight backed up by a backbone of just the right amount of acidity. This is an alluring, floral, and aromatic wine that is not fatiguing; it is versatile and could be paired with dinner fare or enjoyed as a dessert wine.

Chardonnay, I like the versatility of Chardonnay. And they take advantage of this classic grape. I've tried two of their Chardonnays, the steel fermented style and oak aged on the lees style. Go no further; these are benchmarks for site-specific, handcrafted Chardonnay from the Shenandoah Valley AVA and Virginia.

The minerality, balance, and acidity of these are what get me. The steel-fermented Chard is clean and would cut through any white sauce like a knife or balance out a creamy cheese. The oaked Chardonnay is what I want, aged on the lees in French oak barrels; it brings out a classic weightiness of elegance that only Chardonnay can deliver without giving up the acidic structure.

Rockbridge, V d'Or.

This is a must-try dessert wine. It has all the right parts in all the right places to hit every sensory receptor. The aromas of citrus, as in oranges, and the richness of waxy honeycomb and honey drip from your glass. This is an irresistible wine.

Southern Virginia

Rosemont, Sparkling White.

This is a dry sparkling wine with soft, frothy bubbles that immediately salute you in your glass, and it's followed by a unique combination of the aromas of stone fruit, as in peaches, with of squirt of citrus. It finishes with a honed acidity that makes you want more—a great example of what Virginia can do with sparkling wine.

I set out on interview excursions throughout Virginia wine country, visiting as many AVAs as possible and interviewing winery owners and winemakers. Among our excellent winemakers and owners, I found viticulturists, oenologists, agrarians, biochemists, entrepreneurs, husband-and-wife teams, families, jack-of-all-trades, historians, and ex-government employees.

My interviews were straightforward; I asked the **same six questions** to all. In addition, I asked questions based on researching the interviewees. The questions are:

Why do you do what you do?

What has changed in the Virginia wine industry?

What do you want for Virginia wine?

What do you want for the Virginia wine industry?

What are you doing now that excites you?

What do you like wine lovers to know about your wine?

Maya Hood White, winemaker at Early Mountain Vineyards.

From an early age, Maya Hood White was introduced to wine through her family; in my opinion, the best place to learn to enjoy wine. She came to the point of asking, who makes wine? And realizing she wanted to know more, doors of opportunity opened for employment with Afton Mountain Vineyards in Afton, Virginia, where she worked two back-to-back vintages starting in 2009. From this point, Maya moved west to attend U.C. Davis, near Sacramento, California, where she earned a Master of Science (M.S.) degree in Viticulture and Oenology. Thankfully, Maya has returned to Virginia.

Maya oversees the vineyards and supports wine production at Early Mountain Vineyards in Madison, Virginia. Being a viticulturist and oenologist gives her a unique perspective of knowing wine growing from field to table. This combination of intertwined but unique disciplines also helps detect issues and solve vineyard and winemaking problems.

During my days as a hiring manager and interviewing hundreds of candidates, I realized how to recognize people who have discovered their calling by asking what they love to do. And what do their friends, family, or associates say they are good at doing? The response can reveal talented people who have discovered their gift, their calling. Hearing Maya's reactions, I knew she loved her work; check! And she is incredibly good at what she does. A fact supported by winning a gold medal in the 2021 Virginia Governor's Cup competition with *Series 1*, a sweet dessert-style wine. Check number two!

Maya's *Series 1* blends two grapes, Petit Manseng and Malvasia Bianca. Two grapes Maya loves growing due to their synergy with Virginia's climate and growing conditions. Maya had her eye on Petit Manseng and Malvasia Bianca with sweet wine in mind. She then used the appassimento method, an ancient and exciting way of preparing grapes for making wine. The grapes become raisin-like by drying them on mats or hanging them to allow maximum airflow reducing their moisture content by almost half. They are pressed, and the juice is sweet and concentrated, producing this expressive white-sweet blend.

Other styles of wine Maya envisions making are Orange Wine or a Pét-Nat wine using Malvasia Bianca grapes. Orange Wine is made in a red wine fashion by letting the fresh grape juice stay in contact with the grape skins longer than usual for white wine. This gives the wine a redder wine character and an orange tinge. Pét-Nats, short for Pétillant Naturel, is a naturally petillant (bubbly) wine that is slightly sweet, gently fizzy and has low alcohol. As for ideas for other wine styles using the Petit Manseng grape, it would be a dry, lees-aged wine. Lees aging leaves the yeast cells that cause fermentation in contact with the wine for extended periods, creating creamy textures and desirable bread-like or yeasty aromas.

Maya's response was music to my ears when I asked what had changed in the Virginia wine industry. She said people now seek exceptional sites for planting vineyards, thus creating site-specific wine. This concept is encapsulated in terroir, a simple but profound concept. Terroir is the sum of all local wine-making conditions; it includes soil type, weather conditions, topography, vineyard location, and winemaking techniques.

I asked Maya how she keeps herself challenged over time. She described the day-to-day decisions she faces due to Virginia's variation in climate, vineyard duties, challenges with blending wine, her side projects, and more. I realized Maya loves her work and the challenges she faces. And I have never met a person in love that is bored. They are engaged, interested, and busy caring for the object of their affection; this is the sense I got from Maya.

I love asking what three red and white grapes show promise for wine production in Virginia. Seldom is the response kept to just three grapes, which is interesting. I interpret this as Virginia winegrowers thinking extensively about new and exciting wines. As for Maya's reds, Cabernet Franc, Tannat, and Merlot make her list. As for whites Petit Manseng, Chardonnay, Albariño, and Sauvignon Blanc.

What do you want for Virginia wine?

Paraphrasing Maya's response was for Virginia wine to receive its deserved recognition! Ask for nothing more; accept nothing less. That is the sense I got as she explained her perspective. And what better way to gain respect and recognition than by dispensing Virginia wine outside its borders? Maya's vision for Virginia wine is to go global, an idea I should have shared. As she made her case that Virginia deserved recognition for the high quality and exciting things it does with wine, I changed my mind. This was a contagious concept to be understood, communicated, and executed. Get the keys; we're going global!

For this interview, I met Bob Rupy at his winery on the steep slopes of his vineyard in beautiful Bluemont, Virginia. Bob and his wife Loree, owner-operators of October One Vineyard (O1V), started an entrepreneurial venture to make premium wine. When seeking to start a business with a challenge, to grow that business, the committed duo, with help from friends and networking with local winegrowers as in the ever-present Doug Fabbioli. O1V has achieved its goal. This can be seen in the numerous awards, such as in 2021, winning the Loudoun Wine Award's *Chairman's Grand Award* for their 2020 Viognier, plus gold and silver medals for their Merlot and Cabernet Sauvignon.

Customers can find Bob and Loree at local farmer's markets, online, and at their tasting shop in downtown Leesburg Virginia. And the experience of knowing and interacting with the owner-operators of a local winery producing delicious single-vineyard, single-varietal wine rings true to O1V's customers. Their fine wines are made by Walsh Family Wines in Purcellville, Virginia.

When asked what they want wine lovers to know about your wine, the answer was that they offer single-varietal wine made entirely from grapes grown on their land in Bluemont. A single-varietal wine is made from only one grape type. For example, O1V's Albariño is made from 100% Albariño grapes, and their Cabernet Franc is made from 100% Cabernet Franc grapes.

Wine needs enough essential components to please our taste, smell, and tactile receptors. So, wines are blended for a reason, usually to add components not fully available in one grape type. Components such as fruit aromas, grape tannin, acid, and body. There is nothing wrong with blended wine; most wines we enjoy are blends. However, producing wine with enough of the essential pleasing components with one grape type allows an alluring sense of purity in enjoyment. This is how I view O1V's wine.

When asked what has changed in the Virginia wine industry, Bob observed that more thoughtful planning with a better understanding of good vineyard sites is occurring. This versus just planting grapes as an agricultural venture to make money.

I always want to know what keeps winegrowers excited about their work; what keeps them engaged and progressing. A common thread I hear is that there is never a dull moment. Bob put it as well as one can when saying the vintage moves around me, it's dynamic, very different year to year, and the changes fill the void naturally.

When asked what he wants for Virginia wine, another common theme emerges among winegrowers: getting beyond our borders and having it well known that Virginia is making great wine and has a sense of place, a real place with talented people. As for Bob's desire for the Virginia wine industry at large, he wishes for it to embrace new products and to be dynamic while maintaining a grasp of what makes it work.

Bob's advice to young aspiring winegrowers is to make time among all their duties for education. Continuously educate yourself on what's new and changing. Establish trust among your fellow wine industry folks. Contribute to others while moving your business forward and putting some of your energy back into the industry.

Bob said Merlot, Cab Franc, and Cabernet Sauvignon are the three red grapes that show promise. Merlot at O1V thrives with low amounts of grape loss and nicely reflects the nature of a vintage year. Cab Franc always does well in Virginia, and you can bet it will continue improving. Like the Loire Valley in France, it is a staple in Virginia, and local wine lovers expect well-crafted Cab Francs when visiting local wineries.

Cabernet Sauvignon does well in Virginia in a good year and under the right conditions, as in 2010, 2015, and 2017. It is a late-ripening grape, so if the nights are cool and the days are warm in September and October, it shines through in the wine.

Bob's choice of three whites that show promise in Virginia started with Albariño. This grape is a native of Portugal and Spain but was made famous by Portuguese Vinho Verde; translated directly, it means "green wine," but the concept is a young wine intended to be consumed as soon as it is bottled.

The other whites he likes are Sauvignon Blanc and Viognier. These are now part of the fabric of Virginia wine, and we must strive to make the best ones possible. Virginia Sauvignon Blancs are delicious and can compete with New Zealand or California wines head-to-head. Viognier is not the easiest grape to grow, with variability in grape yields, so we must strive to make the best we can, as in O1V's 2020 gold medal winner.

Doug Fabbioli, owner, and winemaker of Fabbioli
Cellars, taps into an inner voice that brings out energetic,
artistic creativity propelling him forward. His desire to get
deeper into the wine industry led him to work at a winery in
New York State, then at the famous Buena Vista Winery in
Sonoma, California, and finally back east to Virginia. After a
stint at Tarara Winery, Doug created Fabbioli Cellars in
Leesburg, Virginia, over twenty years ago.

Doug makes wine for everyone's taste; his enterprise
manages five vineyards and makes thirty types of wine,
including fruit wines. The famous wine writer Oz Clarke once
tasted a Fabbioli pear port made in Doug's Solara system. He
admired it and commented that it reminded him of his

grandmother's wines in Normandy, a region known for fruit wines, cheese, and Calvados, the apple liquor.

Doug is preparing the next generation by teaching wine-growing and rural life skills. He also has an eye for keeping Loudoun's land for agriculture-related businesses and agrotourism, which has led him to be deeply involved with the New Ag School (NAS). NAS offers certificates to all ages to support Loudoun County agribusiness, management, to sales. NAS promotes a love for hands-on learning and a passion for preserving Loudoun County's land.

When answering what is changing in the Virginia wine industry, he said he and peer winegrowers share a mindset that they want to make high-quality wine. Doug pointed out that the Virginia wine industry did not have to transition from a bulk or jug wine culture. Instead, it started further up the quality spectrum and has steadily improved its wine, as he said, "fighting the quality battle every day." According to Doug, Virginia wine is well past first base and consistently makes high-quality wine.

When asked what excites you about winemaking? Doug explained that he operates on the principle of using what you have. This leads Fabbioli Cellars to create exciting styles using Virginia-successful hybrids such as Chambourcin and Vidal Blanc to make rosés, sparkling wines, and barrel-aged wine or for use in blends. Petit Manseng shows promise; despite its tendency towards low grape yields and high acid/pH, this grape can be used across various styles. Tannat, a grape that has won Fabbioli Cellars awards, is exciting in the hands of someone like Doug, who knows how to tame it with suitable barrels for aging.

The next question I posed was, should Virginia have a signature grape? Doug's answer was "No." Should Loudoun County have a signature grape? Again "No." Doug's perspective is that Virginia has many wine cultures, and the diversity of wine is our signature. Instead of a signature grape, we concluded that Virginia might want to lead with a wine type, perhaps Bordeaux blends. Some Virginia wineries already make incredible award-winning Bordeaux blends; others leverage the Meritage Alliance marketing and labeling concept. Another grape to lead with could be the ever-present-in-Virginia, Cabernet Franc. Doug refers to Virginia Cab Francs as expressing a Pinot-plus character and, in his side-by-side tastings, says they stand up to Cab Francs from its home in the Loire Valley, France.

When asked what he would tell a rising wine professional, Doug responded, "Learn from experienced people but know your mentor's strengths." He said to determine if your mentor is a businessperson. Or people person? Or winemaker? Also, be humble and listen. Once engaged, get to know your supporting cast, the vineyard crew, for example. As for this tidbit of advice, I know from tasting at Fabbioli Cellars that the popular and yummy Paco Rojo was blended with input from his field hands. His other wisdom, serving a bad wine in a tasting lineup diminishes the customer's experience, so concentrate on quality, quality, and quality; it will preserve your brand's reputation.

What do you want from the Virginia wine industry was addressed with, make more wine, enough to get into the wholesale market, perhaps with a consistently high-quality grape as in Cabernet Franc or Chambourcin. Move beyond the cottage industry, make more significant volumes of wine, and move beyond the Virginia borders with wine and a reputation for quality.

Robbie Corpora, the winemaker at Ramiiisol Vineyards, submitted the following responses to the six questions.

Why do you do what you do?

"It was Jefferson's dream to produce world-class wines, so the mission at Ramiiisol is accomplishing Jefferson's dream, the production of natural world-class wines that exhibit place and are grounded in our local terroir and climate. And to do it organically without the use of synthetic products."

What has changed in the Virginia wine industry since you began?

"Significant growth. More producers, grapes, varieties, and wines are being produced in Virginia now than ever. Still, much of the industry follows a similar model, often looking to Bordeaux and Napa to decide which grapes to grow and how to produce the wine. So, despite the great diversity, we are experiencing a somewhat homogenous evolution."

What do you want for the Virginia wine industry?

"I would like to see the Monticello AVA gaining notoriety as a top-quality wine-producing region in the world, where a consumer can come to understand the distinct personalities of our region and how it is expressed in wines that are of equal and sometimes greater quality than many of the great wines in the world. For me, I already see a lifetime of exploration possible with the variety of expressions of Cabernet Franc in our various soils and climates just on our small farm at Ramiiisol. Imagine the possibilities in the rest of the Monticello AVA."

What do you want for Virginia wine?

"I hope to see a greater degree of two things: 1. Emphasis on personality: meaning let's stop making Meritage style wine and make Monticello style wine that is nothing but an expression of Monticello rather than an attempt to emulate another region; 2. Focus: with so many varieties in our vineyards and so many wines in our tasting rooms; I find it difficult to believe that any producer can truly focus on producing the best of the best."

What are you doing now that excites you?

"There is nothing we do that doesn't excite us here at Ramiiisol. Every vintage, every day, is an experiment, and the results are never easy to interpret. Careful observation is a continuing obsession."

What do you like wine lovers to know about your wine?

"While it is always evolving in both the bottle and the glass, it is impossible to say exactly what we "know" as what we experience today may be further developed next year. We believe the essential thing for wine lovers is to enjoy their personal experience of the moment with our wines.

That said, it is essential to understand that we are raising our vines in a humid and passionate climate. As our consultant, Alberto Antonini, pointed out, our terratorium's atmosphere gives us "filtered light, " giving birth to great elegance and complexity."

How would you explain biodynamic viticulture to Caleb, my nine-year-old grandson?

"Hello, Caleb; Biodynamics is very simple. Please think of the ocean and how it moves. Now imagine how that same movement exists in all natural things, breathing in and out like the waves crash and return. Biodynamics is carefully observing these rhythms and fine-tuning your wine growing work to take advantage of them--- to work less and to achieve more."

What is one unexpected outcome you discovered from biodynamic viticulture?

"Even ultra-cosmic compost teas will fry your cell phone if you drop it in the bucket while dynamizing. I have found that biodynamic agriculture is much simpler and easier to execute than expected. To many, it all seems far-fetched and a little crazy. Still, careful observation over the years tells us that the overriding principles hold together and are a powerful, logical way of following nature's rhythms. As our terroir consultant, Pedro Parra, said, "The terroir gives place to the wine; biodynamics adds a mysterious energy to the wine."

When interviewing Jon Wehner, the owner and winemaker of Chatham Creek Vineyard, I felt as if I was talking to one of our independent spirited forefathers who was granted land on Virginia's eastern shore from the King of England.

To sustain his livelihood, a man had to learn all the aspects of an agrarian existence while relying on family bonds and interdependent relationships with neighbors.

At other points, it was as if I was attending a master's class in the philosophy of wine. Drawing from his childhood experience, we covered everything from starting and sustaining a successful wine business to the long-term management of a winery, climate conditions, site selection, clone selection, harvest concepts, and more.

Jon's response to my first question, "Why do you do what you do?" was, "Ultimately, its quality of life and sustainability." With these goals in mind, he began a journey of thoughtful progress that began early in childhood.

Jon's father worked in Washington D.C. and had a twenty-acre farm in Fairfax County, Virginia, including an experimental vineyard. Jon lived through harvests, raising cattle and horses, gardening, and tending the family garden and orchards of peaches, apples, and grapes. He enjoyed their neighbors, the country lifestyle, and the "life with happiness," as he put it. The agrarian lifestyle became part of Jon.

The path of thoughtful progress

Jon's path took him through a short office career, and after moving to the eastern shore, he took what he learned from his upbringing and used it as a foundation when developing Chatham Vineyards twenty-five years ago.

Jon started research for Chatham Vineyards in the late nineties, working with vineyard consultant Lucy Morton. Then on to Virginia wine industry leaders Linden Vineyards, and Barboursville, for its viticultural practices.

At first, Jon concentrated on growing high-quality wine grapes to be a large-scale grape producer for Virginia wineries. Once achieving his first goal, a natural progression occurred to sustain and diversify Chatham's business by making wine.

With winemaking in mind, from 2002 to 2005, he made private-label wine while gaining experience with his vineyard and understanding its flavor profiles. Then in 2005, he started Chatham Vineyards, planting large acreage up front, not concentrating on buildings or a big winery. All the while, he continued to sell grapes to other vineyards.

The next step came from the need to distribute Chatham's wine. So, he and his wife Mills started Eastern Shore Classic Wines a year before the state of Virginia created the Virginia Wine Distribution Company (VWDC).

Today Chatham Vineyards produces three to five thousand cases of wine annually. Its European-style vineyards contain thirty-two thousand vines of Chardonnay, Cabernet Franc, Cabernet Sauvignon, Merlot, and Petit Verdot—the winery employees state of the art equipment, quality-controlled vineyard management, and hand harvesting and sorting. Grapes not vinified at the winery are sold to other wineries in Virginia.

They have two styles of Chardonnay, oak aged and steel fermented; both are made with 100% Chardonnay. Their dry Church Creek Rosé is a fifty-fifty Merlot and Cabernet Franc blend. They have two single-varietal wines from Merlot and Cabernet Franc and a Bordeaux blend. The blend is a Bordeaux blend called Vintner's Blend and is made from Petit Verdot, Merlot, Cabernet Sauvignon, and Cabernet Franc. To round out their offerings nicely, Chatham makes a red, late-harvest dessert wine with 3% residual sugar.

Jon said that every twenty-three vintages have been unique since starting. His philosophy of wine always comes with time, experience, and the need to experiment and change techniques. He says this is a slow, subtle business with no shortcuts, no way to buy your way through the challenges or its natural evolution.

What has changed in the Virginia wine industry since you began?

Growth. Being engaged for over two decades and he experienced growth from sixty wineries to over three hundred plus wineries across Virginia. He lived through the experimentation phase in Virginia and saw tremendous improvements in wine quality, with more consistent wine now being made.

Jon says now, "Virginia wines are more consistent and identifiable. For example, Virginia chardonnay is now recognizable as a Virginia wine, and so is Cabernet Franc. Virginia makes unique, distinct, and interesting wines. Most people did not know where their wine came from in the past, but now they are proud to drink local and regional wines and support small and homegrown businesses."

What do you want for the Virginia wine industry?

Authenticity. Do not try to emulate anything. Continue to develop Virginia's wine identity. Don't strive for something we are not. For consumers to view us in the context of Virginia, not comparing us to California, for example.

North to south, east to west, explore and embrace the diversity of Virginia terroir and communicate that through our wine. And don't become a one-grape state. Grape types used should be as diverse as the terroir. Don't market a single grape type. Experiment to get to the next level with the quality of our wine.

On a maturity curve, Jon likened the Virginia wine industry to someone in their twenties. The world is ahead of them. They have their education. They have their essential experiences. They are free thinkers that are going to chart their course. It's a powerful place to be when you have the most freedom of your life and are hungry for more, with so much potential and opportunity for growth.

He continued, "With support from the Virginia state government, we must allow ourselves to experiment and produce unique wine that varies year to year, highlighting the climate and winemakers' adaptability and skill. Not to try to make predictable wines, but distinct wine."

What do you want for Virginia wine?

Virginia offers boundless assets and opportunities in a diversity of terroir. The Virginia wine industry must evolve and encourage experimentation. Winemaking should not be limited to one region of the state. Virginians should make unique wines from the coast to the mountains.

What are you doing now that excites you about wine?

Chatham Vineyards is at a pivotal moment in its lifecycle. This leads to redevelopment using knowledge gained from over two decades of experience.

This is like a second go-round, with more vineyard site knowledge, looking to the next generation, giving them the knowledge not available when Chatham Vineyards was started.

Decisions were initially made upfront with a limited amount of info and understanding of our site, which had never grown grapes. As a result, you have twenty to forty years of living with decisions made without experience and practical knowledge.

Now we know what works. Now we see what we have, what has been successful, which clones, which varietals we used, and we're redeveloping with new clones, varietals, and vine spacing.

For example, Petit Verdot, clone #400, was initially used as a blending grape. It is austere, but we're going with a new clone, Petit Verdot French clone #1058, it's more subtle and elegant, and this may lead to a single varietal line of wine.

We will employ Riparia rootstock; it has less canopy, reducing hand work in the vineyard. With Virginia's rainfall, a less vigorous, slower-growing rootstock would be helpful.

We are adding more Chardonnay, seeing our current steel fermented sells out annually. The steel Chardonnay is an incredible wine, Chatham's most expressive, identifiable wine, and we want more. This is a high-acid wine, fruit-forward, lean, and angular.

It's minerally with a saline quality from the ocean influence. It has tremendous fruit from the first-generation French clones, good viticulture practices, and the moderate maritime climate of the Eastern Shore, with deep soils and marine deposits from shells. It complements our barrel-fermented Chardonnay, which has riper fruit, lower acid, and ages in French oak.

Subtle corrections are being made. Based on the current success with French Dijon clones #95, #96, and especially #76, we are planting more acreage of clone #76. In addition, we will introduce clone #548, an early ripening clone with a slightly different flavor profile. This will allow for multiple harvests due to the ripeness windows of the different clones, reducing the risks of weather events damaging the grapes.

Petit Verdot, a new target, is possibly making a single varietal wine, not with clone #400, as previously, but clone #1058, with three-year-old American oak barrels made by Canton Cooperage in Lebanon, Kentucky. Certain grape types will work with American oak, and Petit Verdot won't be overpowered by it.

What do you like wine lovers to know about you or your wine?

We produce a great wine on Virginia's eastern shore. Our wines are distinct, intriguing, and site-specific, reflecting Chatham Vineyards and Virginia's Eastern Shore.

Consumers want unique wine, and Virginia makes that type of wine. It does not make daily drinking wine; it makes specialty, handmade wines.

Virginia's style of wine is closer to European wine. However, Virginia's wine is its own; we make a medium body, elegant wines that are great with food; they are austere and restrained.

Chatham's climate is not like California's. It's night and day different. For example, California gets nine to twelve inches of rain; in Virginia, we get more than fifty inches yearly. So, it is more like Europe in that sense.

Virginia has non-predictable wine that varies with the natural climate changes. A wine that doesn't please anyone and doesn't offend anyone; those are the wines of other places.

Our steel-fermented Chardonnay is one of Virginia's most recognizable site-expressive wines. People ask what its secret is. The secret is that it's made in the vineyard. But we whole cluster press our Chardonnay and have a minimalist wine-making approach using French clones, rootstock, and special trellising. It's a combination of all these things, not just one thing.

Also, Chatham Vineyards is a special and unique place in Virginia and America. Millions of Church Creek Cork oysters are cultured three hundred yards from Chatham Vineyards. This is one of the few places in the world with oysters and wine bound by location and climate. They are produced together, making an unforgettable wine and seafood pairing.

The protected waters make for deeper cupped and thicker oyster shells. The saltiness is less pronounced, with hints of seagrass in the finish of these oysters, with enough brine to savor the velvety essence of the Chesapeake.

The Virginia Nature Conservancy owns the woods, the shorelines, and islands around Chatham Vineyards, and you can take kayak tours to experience the beauty of the Virginia shore, end up at our vineyard and taste the essence of the land.

Jon's phrases

I listened to the interview audio with Jon multiple times and realized many topics could be turned into a chapter or books themselves. One aspect that jumped out at me was the phrases Jon used to express himself. They are worthy of capturing. These could be Virginia wine marketing slogans, posters, bumper stickers, or tee shirts!

Winegrowing - there's no way to buy yourself through the challenges.

Virginia wine growing - slow and subtle.

In Virginia wine country, the fast way is the slow way.

Virginia wine - a sense of place.

We know who we are – Virginia Wine!

Virginia, our winegrowers play the long game.

Sorry, no instant gratification with Virginia wine.

In Virginia, the weather is the great equalizer.

Virginia grape growers complain less than farmers.

Kent Ardent – Winemaker, Walsh Family Wine

Why do you do what you do?

I caught the wine bug about ten years ago and kept digging deeper down that rabbit hole. Seven years ago, I quit my analyst job at the Department of Energy, drove cross country, and took a wine internship at a massive winery in Washington State to see what it was all about.

I've always needed tangible results from my work, and winemaking seemed to combine all the aspects of how I wanted to live my life. I wanted a new lifestyle, a better lifestyle. Unlike farming, wine growing appeals to me; I like the yearly cycle of vineyard work, cellar work, and wine production.

What has changed in the Virginia wine industry?

A lot has changed. Indeed, the varieties we are planting and growing are homing in on the best varieties for our climate, for example, Petit Manseng and Cabernet Franc.

The marketing and agrotourism of today are also vastly different from years ago. It's no secret that wine consumption across the country is slowing, and we are also experiencing that a little bit here in Virginia. I think it's becoming harder to rely on the steady flow of tourism that we have become accustomed to over the past thirty years.

The Virginia wine industry must stay fresh. We must stay relevant to people; keeping them interested in wine and providing a draw is part of our job now.

What are you doing now that excites you?

I am learning new things every year at Walsh Family Wine. From working with new varieties to making wine for clients, learning new winemaking styles and techniques, e.g., force carbing, canning, making cider, Pét-Nats, port-style wine, vermouth, and more.

We now make twenty thousand cases per year. We started at a thousand cases per year. And half of what we do is custom crush for other people. I have opportunities to work with new varieties of grapes and new styles of wine and use new equipment. At one point, we had one-hundred-twenty fermentations going; that happened last year. There's always something new at the Walsh Family winery.

I'm also excited, of course, to have the opportunity to launch my label – *Boden Young*, in 2021. It's remarkable to experiment with the style I like and not necessarily be constrained to the typical formula that most wineries produce under. I like to make wine I drink, and building my brand is exciting. In the future, I'll keep the production to about two to three-hundred cases per year.

How do winemakers keep from getting what is called house-palette or cellar palette?

The phenomenon can occur when you drink your wine and become blind to its faults or shortcomings. Kent said that typically, winemakers graduate to more acidic, less

79

sweet wine. But wine should reflect the winemaker's palate, so how do they keep it from getting too acidic? They must keep tasting wine. Blind taste wine. Try wines in their area—wines from around the world like what they make as a comparison.

What do you want for Virginia wine?

I want Virginia wine to become more recognized for its quality. Also, I'd like the perception of the Virginia wine industry and its reputation to improve. Not the reputation from many years ago for making sweet wine.

And produce better quality wine within its regions, concentrating on grapes that grow well in the vast range of soil types and elevations. Naturally, this would lead to the creation of more appellations, smaller appellations. For example, make one called Catoctin Ridge. Because the wine there is uniquely different, and the fruit is good. So, more appellations in general.

What do you want for the Virginia wine industry?

I'd love for the industry to become more well-known. We are reaching different markets, but the old stereotypes of sweet wines still linger.

What do you want wine lovers to know about your wine?

Appreciate the work that goes into a glass of wine. Winemakers care and speaking not only for myself but for other winemakers/vineyard managers/educators, we put immense effort into making quality wine and growing quality fruit. This could be another interview on this topic alone, but the more significant point I am trying to make is that a lot is happening behind the scenes that the consumer doesn't see.

Long days, early mornings, little sleep, brutal weather, endless work. I sometimes feel like wine consumers' view of wine professionals is that we sit around and drink wine, which is far from the truth. There is a vast disconnect between what the consumers see and the work.

What are your favorite red and white grapes showing promise in Northern Virginia?

Whites: Petit Manseng, it's the star of vinifera for Virginia as far as growing well in our climate. It's disease resistant, with thick skin and high acid. Even in the difficult 2018 season, Petit Manseng did well. The fruit was clean, did not have rot, didn't have canopy issues, ripened, and didn't need sorting.

As for the wine, if you blend this wine, it blends well with Viognier to balance it. It's a versatile grape; you can make any style of wine, from sweet to dry. But you must know how to tame it. Harvesting it early and using skin contact techniques to manage the pH makes excellent wine. Also, you can over-crop it to reduce the grape sugars.

Albariño, it's a close second to Petit Manseng. It has loose clusters, thick skin, low yielding, and smaller clusters. It grows better than Chardonnay and Viognier in our area. The third would be Vermentino, and it's starting to show promise in Virginia.

Reds: Cab Franc, Petit Verdot, and Tannat consistently acclimate to Virginia. These three grapes produce good fruit, creating quality wines.

Cabernet Franc works well in Virginia. It has loose clusters, with thicker skinned berries (grapes), thus reducing disease. It's tamed in the vineyard now as we have gained experience growing it, as early sun exposure ensures it ripens, reducing the greenness and green pepper aromas in the wine.

Petit Verdot does well in our area. It has small berries, does even better when blended, and works well aging in new oak. Tannat, this grape can be site-specific; it's not a cold hardy grape, so in the right spot does well. It also needs the complement of oak aging and lots of aging, ten to fifteen years.

What advice would you give young wine professionals?

Continue to educate yourself and your guests. This is the best way to keep people interested in Virginia wine or any region. Be prepared for vineyard work; it's outside farmwork. And learn how to taste wine better. Be adaptable; every day is going to be different. Many tasks are necessary. You must know how to fix everything, and you're a part-time electrician, plumber, and manager, so learn how to manage people.

Why do you do what you do?

Williamsburg Winery's winemaker Matthew Meyer was introduced to wine by his father, a wine lover, and it became a part of his life from childhood. While in college in Washington D.C. and studying international relations and public policy with the end goal of becoming a diplomat, he was influenced by friends to change course.

His peers observed him hosting wine events and starting a wine club and noticed his knowledge and keen interest in wine. As a result, his peers encouraged him to return to California and attend UC Davis, study wine, and make his hobby his career!

After contacting UC Davis and speaking to the famous Ann Noble, a sensory chemist and professor in the Department of Viticulture and Oenology, he pursued the study of wine. Ann Noble is the inventor of the *Aroma Wheel*, credited with enhancing the public's understanding of wine tasting and terminology.

Winemakers are always deeply connected to the farming end of wine. And as Matthew said, "The more I got into it, I liked the farming aspect. I like taking an agricultural product, a grape, and you nurture it every year and squish them, and from grapes out in the vineyard to a finished product, it's fascinating. What you see in the vineyard, the grapes, and you picture in a few years will be on someone's shelf, cellar, or dining room table. Someone's going to be enjoying that wine."

Great things can be achieved by people such as Williamsburg Winery founder Patrick Duffeler, and Matthew Meyer, people with vision, expertise, and drive. And recognizing that a sense of place is a large part of a wine's allure and significant to consumers and winegrowers,

Williamsburg Winery spearheaded forming and establishing an American Viticultural Area (AVA).

On September 24, 2021 the U.S. government approved the Virginia Peninsula AVA, the eighth official wine-growing region in Virginia. Williamsburg Winery's team worked on this long and time-consuming project. The Alcohol and Tobacco Tax and Trade Bureau (TTB) awards an AVA to winegrowing regions with discrete attributes and geographically defined boundaries.

The data required by the government as part of the approval process includes historical references of the proposed AVA name, in this case, Virginia Peninsula. Also, climate data, elevation, geology, latitude, soil makeup, sun coverage, and topographic anatomy! Everything related to winegrowing is examined before a request is submitted and approved through the TTB.

As the AVA was unfolding, Matthew Meyer said, "I remember years ago studying geological survey maps trying to figure out where we would start," upon approval, Meyer said,

"This news validates that Virginia continues to be up and coming in the wine world. It validates that we have a unique terroir here and unique growing conditions. It's a huge deal for labeling. For example, we will be able to label our wines as "Estate Grown" and "Estate Bottled."" The next steps will be building a sense of community within the Virginia Peninsula AVA, perhaps with a wine trail for promotion and cross-marketing.

What do you want for the Virginia wine industry?

Do not focus on one or two grape types as a state. We should avoid the notion of Cabernet Franc and Viognier as our state grapes; it's unnecessary. Virginia makes so many wines, and grapes are well suited for Virginia. For example, Petit Verdot, Albariño, and Petit Manseng.

Broader distribution of Virginia wine so consumers can get our wine, both inside and beyond Virginia. And the key to this is more land dedicated to growing grapes and more mechanized farming. Also, it would be helpful for Virginia restaurants and businesses to realize the quality of our wine and integrate it into their offerings, equal to and alongside all the other wines.

What do you want for Virginia wine?

Experimentation to determine what grapes grow well in Virginia. How about experimentation with grapes from Northern Spain and Portugal? Albariño, Garnacha, Tempranillo for example. And the Rkatsiteli grape from the Republic of Georgia makes excellent wine that Williamsburg wine club members love.

As winemakers, we must continue to make the best wine possible. This has already yielded positive results in national and international wine competitions. For example, Williamsburg Winery's 2019 Wessex Hundred Viognier received 93 points and a Gold Medal in the 2021 Winemaker Challenge International Wine Competition. The 2019 Viognier is made from grapes grown in the Virginia Peninsula AVA.

We need a greater depth of marketing for Virginia wine with a long-term perspective. Also, we must reach a younger demographic; the competition from spirits, cocktails, and microbrews is making the Virginia wine industry need to step up its marketing.

Compared to beer and spirits, the Virginia wine industry is outspent. A collective approach to marketing Virginia wine would help. At one point, Williamsburg Winery organized a well-received tasting in London, England. More of this type of concept would be helpful. This could be done locally as well, throughout Virginia.

What are you doing now that excites you?

I am excited about Albariño. This is partly based on love for this grape, customer feedback, and analysis of NASA satellite data. NASA approached us to consult on a research project they were doing. NASA researchers mapped Virginia meter by meter via satellite, gathering atmospheric conditions, slope, topography, etc. And what we compared to the closest is Northern Spain. This convinced me even more, to pursue Albariño on a larger scale. This is exciting to me.

What do you want people to know about your wine?

Virginia, better than anywhere in the world, blends the New World and the Old World concerning wine. It's a perfect combination of both. I like that a lot since I grew up in the Old World.

I strive for balance, elegance, and layers in my wine. Also, producing food-friendly wine pleases people, leaving them wanting more.

We have one thing we should talk more about that nobody has: it's the Chesapeake Bay. The aquaculture is unique to us; I want my wine to go with the oysters, the fish, the clams, and anything that walks, crawls, or creeps out of that Chesapeake Bay. That is something that Virginia truly owns.

What three red and white grapes show promise in Virginia?

First, speaking in broad terms, I work with Vitis Vinifera grapes and prefer them. But as for hybrids, I like, there is Chambourcin; it can be made in many styles. Hybrids can be bulletproof; they have good grape yields and are disease- and bug-resistant. Also, the white Chardonel grape, a cross of a French American hybrid Seyval with Chardonnay, make good wine.

As for non-Vinifera, non-hybrid grapes Norton, if done well, is stunning. I tried a Loxley Reserve from Chrysalis; it had some age on it and was like a good Bordeaux. I make mine with a touch of Petit Verdot and use good French barrels with excellent outcomes.

As for my favorite Vitis Vinifera grapes, Petit Verdot, Tannat should be focused on. And possibly Tempranillo has potential; it needs more exposure in Virginia, so it may be too early to tell, but it's on my radar. And Merlot, it's a forgotten grape that should be revitalized. It does very well in our climate and impressed me when coming here from California.

As for whites, Petit Manseng and Albariño, I think, are going to take off. Also, Sauvignon Blanc, there are some promises there too. Mainly if we make them in the Old-World style, they are lovely. The Rkatsiteli grape, I enjoy making a dry-style wine with this grape. And as I mentioned, the response from our wine club members is very optimistic about Rkatsiteli.

Acte 12 of 1619 Chardonnay

In the early 1600s, after attempts failed at winemaking from native vines, the English colonists imported various French vines. The first legislative assembly of the New World, the House of Burgesses, passed *Acte 12*, which required every male household in Virginia to plant ten vines of imported vinifera grapes in order to make wine. John Johnson, one of the first settlers, exceeded the law's requirements by planting eighty-five acres on Williamsburg Winery's property. The vineyard honors these attempts with their *Acte 12 of 1619* Chardonnay.

Owner and winemaker Kerem Baki met in his office at Hillsborough Winery.

Why do you do what you do?

In my senior year at Virginia Tech, during my undergraduate degree, I took a wine appreciation course called Wines and Vines, taught by Dr. Bruce Zoecklein, the Virginia state oenologist. I was studying biochemistry then, and it sounded like a fun course. At that time, my father retired and was looking for a new hobby, and he was interested in starting a vineyard, like an acre, for fun to play with.

Meanwhile, I enjoyed the wine course and found that what I studied in biochemistry could be applied to winemaking and grape growing, and the semester ended with an option for a six-month internship, which I took at Chrysalis Vineyards in Middleburg, Virginia. This was a perfect place for me since owner and winemaker Jenny McCloud had set up a research vineyard with over twenty grape varieties to see what would grow well. She worked with great winemakers such as Alan Kenny and consulted with other high-profile individuals at the time, including Dr. Bruce Zoecklein, who helped establish her project.

After a year at Chrysalis Vineyards, my father and I planned to grow his acre vineyard project and make a go of it. Meanwhile, I returned to Virginia Tech to obtain a Masters's in Oenology, studying under Dr. Bruce Zoecklein and working with Tony Wolf at his viticulture site.

After finishing the oenology program, my father and I expanded our vineyard to six acres at first and then eight, and now we are maxed out at fourteen. We now grow 100% of our grapes here at Hillsborough Winery and make all our wine. We can also make wine for other wineries and sell our fruit when we have extra grapes.

I like the science aspect of this work; I love the nature and the farming part. I love the ability to do independent work when I feel like being alone and the opportunity to do teamwork, as in working with the tasting room staff. Then there are social aspects, working with the community and the customers. In Virginia, every growing season is different; the weather throws a new challenge at us every year.

So, in this job, you are growing something from the earth, turning it into something else, and then serving a customer. So, you start from the ground up and, in the end, see the gratification on a person's face and how they like our wine.

This work contains all the aspects of a three-tiered system, production, distribution, and sale of wine. And the beauty is that I can put myself into each of those depending on what needs to be done. That's why I enjoy this job so much.

What has changed in the Virginia wine industry since you began?

Multiple factors have changed; one, the quality of Virginia wine has improved. I remember twenty years ago, Virginia was getting mixed reviews. But we reached a turning point; I noticed it was around two-thousand ten, the quality was better, and everybody was lifting the bar, helping each other to understand it. Also, there have been many programs by Virginia Tech, they have extension programs to teach people what they are seeing because of their research with vines, grapes, and soil, and they are even developing a hybrid grape for the Virginia climate.

Also, our wine industry has shifted to the wine and hospitality industry as of late, and at first curious wine-people visited us for the love of wine, researching our wine, and tasting our wine. We still have wine lovers coming out in more significant numbers, but we also have people coming out to hang out with friends and family at a beautiful location. They want an excellent venue to enjoy the view and food with our wine. So, our industry has evolved.

The advantage of the wine-hospitality industry is that we have direct contact with our customers and can focus on our messaging. We can explain Hillsborough Winery's wine's quality, distinction, and characteristics. This allows us to focus on grapes and wine we like and do well at our site and not be forced to focus on what is popular.

Our vineyards have also matured, and we are seeing a better-tasting grape coming out. The older our vineyard gets, the better the grapes, and as a result, our wine is more concentrated; it has more depth of flavor. For example, we are now making Tannat from twenty-year-old vines, and I see a clear difference, and improvement, from our earlier vintages.

Additionally, our vineyard soil has been mined over the years by the grapevine varieties we planted. In our case, the farm here was a cattle farm, so we had plenty of nitrogen. In some cases, cover crops can be planted between the rows of vines to remediate the soil to suit the vines better, and to balance nitrogen content, for example.

What do you want for Virginia wine?

Please keep doing what they are doing concerning quality. Learn more about viticulture. Focus on our wine. There is a danger of wineries only expending energy on their hospitality and tasting room, not growing grapes or making wine. The problem arises when they need a distinction, an identity for their wine; their branding will need to expand. Instead, we should establish that our industry is farm-based, the product is grown by us, and our wine must have a distinctive quality so that we can communicate to the consumer to keep their interest peaked.

What do you want for the Virginia wine industry?

More collaboration with businesses. Support from joining industries is essential for growth. We are collaborating with bed and breakfasts, restaurants, and other parts of the tourism industry. But we have not saturated the market to the point of California or France. For example, in California wine country, the overwhelming focus is on their wine; you see it in the forefront of advertisements, prominently on menus, and in stores.

We should focus on making our wine a part of everyday life in Virginia. This can be achieved by growing more fruit, making more wine available, and being price competitive. Then design wine for everyday consumption and various experiences, from casual to fine dining.

Also, it would be beneficial to create regions of distinction for Virginia wine. Not for competition's sake but for marketing and local consumption, to build a connection between locals and their local wine.

In addition, I would like to see the emergence of more grape varieties. More varieties in Virginia and more experimentation. When I started in the early two-thousands, wineries were moving away from planting what was popular and did well in California, particularly Cabernet Sauvignon and Chardonnay. These wines did well on the west coast and sold well in the U.S. market, but these grapes are challenging to grow in Virginia, so wineries looked at other varieties.

Their focus changed to Cabernet Franc and Viognier, which was well received but needed to grow better everywhere in the state. So, we then saw some alternate varieties gaining popularity, like Petit Verdot, Petit Manseng, and Tannat, and then Albariño, Roussanne, Chenin Blanc, and Rkatsiteli. These wines are now growing in popularity and winning accolades in competitions, locally and internationally.

What are you doing now that excites you?

Great wine is made in the vineyard, so I am assessing and understanding my grapes more. I predict how my wine will turn out based on the grape quality coming in from the vineyard and adjust accordingly.

For example, if my grapes are too acidic or sour, I can adjust my growing practices and harvest timing to accommodate that. If my wine is too tannic or a rough mouthfeel, I can adjust that in the winemaking process and the vineyard.

So, what I am ending up creating is a wine that is a direct representation of the vineyard. As opposed to a chemically altered wine in the winery, this way, it's a more natural product, a purer product. The less you add to the wine, the more flavorful and complex it is; you're not stripping anything away. This has been my primary focus, and I get better every year.

What do you like wine lovers to know about your wine?

Our brand is that you can't taste our wine anywhere else. We only use our grapes. Therefore, our wine has a sense of place. It identifies our land, our personalities, and Hillsborough, Virginia. I design my wine and grow my grapes based on the types of food I grew up eating and what I like to eat. If I can create a wine with the distinction that it represents me and my land, I've done it right.

What red grapes show promise in Virginia?

Tannat, Petit Verdot, Chambourcin, and Norton

What white grapes show promise?

Petit Manseng, Sauvignon Blanc, Chenin Blanc

Emily Hodson, head winemaker at Veritas Vineyards.

Why do you do what you do?

Because I fell in love with it, I've always been interested in wine and a foodie. This opportunity fell in my lap; I wasn't looking to be in this field; I was interested in medicine, epidemiology, and the science of disease. This was meant to be. I landed here at a particular time and got involved in planting a vineyard and meeting a very new wine industry. I adored every minute of it, from installing irrigation to planting vines. I still enjoy it; I'm going into my twenty-third vintage and excited; I love it.

I am a wine geek but on the science side of wine. Everything about the science side of wine fits me well. I enjoy it; the more I learn, I realize I have more to learn; it has endless growth potential and development. Every year I have so many more questions and ideas; I find it challenging, stimulating, and gratifying.

To go back to the beginning, I was working for Save the Children in Southeast Asia for the CDC. I needed a break from work, and my parents had just bought this property, and I was taking time off to see where I was going next. And there were clear signs that I was supposed to stay in Afton, Virginia, which I doubted at first, if not for anything else, just the contrast of where I had lived, Atlanta and Jacksonville.

As for the "why me?", I think this was just timing; I was at the right age, in the right frame of mind, when my family started this venture. But the additional context of my earlier life comes into play.

I have always had a very sensitive smell recall, which I never understood until I started working professionally with smells associated with wine.

Also, my dad is a Francophile, he's English, and all our vacations were centered around wine regions, learning about wine, and collecting wine. So, this is one of the passions of my dad's life. This is his second career; they moved to Afton specifically for this. I don't know if they envisioned it would get this big or that the whole family would be involved as we are now. My brother, sister, her husband, the assistant winemaker, and my uncle, the vineyard manager, all work here. Now we are a multigeneration, multilayer family business. And so, it keeps growing, and I think the next chapter will be more interesting, you know, our kids, having grown up in it, in a way my brother, sister, and I didn't. They've grown up on the vineyard. We each have two girls, so our folks have six grand girls aged 3 to 17.

And the influence of my mom comes into play; she has a green thumb and can grow anything, and she has come to love farming as I have; I think she fell in love with it after they got their first twenty acres of vines in the ground.

Also, the people in this industry are excellent; it's a great field to work in; we learn from each other, grow with each other, and we all have the same mindset in farming, production, and food, so I enjoy my peers. And that has been a big part of my experience.

What has changed in the Virginia wine industry since you began?

I will start with the vineyard and what we are growing; now, we are doing a much better job of canopy maintenance and looking at balance and vine health. The plant material we buy has increased in quality from what was available in the early days.

We are gaining more focus on not just planting, not just what we want on the land we have, but looking at what grapes are well suited and finding areas that are good grape growing areas. I have noticed; that fewer people are planting on Grandpa's farm just because they have the land; now, for example, they are looking through the Shenandoah Valley, looking at soil types, and scouring maps to find great spots to grow grapes. That has been a significant change in our industry.

And clonal awareness has changed; for example, if you plan to plant Sauvignon Blanc, you can select a well-suited clone for your site. A clone with open grape clusters or more extended cluster stems that hang off the vine, enabling more wind flow. So, now we order grapes more purposefully.

What do you want for Virginia wine?

I want Virginia wine to get outside of Virginia. That is something I feel very passionate about. That means I want more vines in the ground. That's the only way I know of solving this. The business model of agrotourism is great, but for the long-term success of the wine industry, we need to be on more wine lists and have more consumer awareness.

I want us to be part of the understood conversation about wine. We have made a lot of progress, especially on the East Coast. So, working on improving our wine presence even more on the East Coast and the South, being a part of

Southern food culture, and becoming more of a day-to-day experience, not a day-trip experience.

What do you want for the Virginia wine industry?

Grape breeding within the Vinifera species of grapes. I want to start reducing how much we must go through the vineyard, maintenance, less tractor work, etc. Fewer inputs in the vineyards, less diesel fuel, and fewer chemicals.

If I were queen of Virginia wine, I would edict at least two acres of land for new grape evaluation, which would be repeated every five years. Every vineyard would commit land to evaluate grape varieties. More grapes in the ground would increase production throughout the state, allowing us to keep evaluating and fine-tuning what grapes work well here, which require less spraying and less diesel fuel. The hard part of breeding is that it's a long-term project. It is a constant query of what grows best all over Virginia. If we keep planting the same five grapes, we'll never know the best grapes for each region.

I am not alone; I have comrades working on this, Ben Jordan, Ruth Saunders at Silver Creek, Maya Hood White,

Ben Sedlins from Walsh Family Wine, and Dr. Lance Cadle-Davidson, a Research Plant Pathologist at the USDA Grape Genetics Research Unit (GGRU) at Cornell University, Geneva, NY.

What are you doing now that excites you?

Working with the Winemakers Research Exchange (WRE), the WRE started as a group of winemakers in Monticello doing experiments in our cellars. And about six years ago, the Virginia Wine Board (VWB) wanted to foster this by funding us and setting up scientifically sound experiments.

From a winemaking perspective, we are from all over the place and have different winemaking techniques. The WRE has raised our collective curiosity and understanding about doing things better in the cellar. Whether that's no sulfites, skin contact, or lowering sulfite while looking at tannin additions or a hundred other benefits, it's the evaluation of precisely what we can do to grow and make Virginia wine that is best for Virginia wine.

Because we all started learning from the West Coast and Europe, that is an excellent place to start, but the context of Virginia makes for different grapes. Even though we are growing many of the same grapes, our pH levels are different, our humidity is different, and our phenological ripening is different. So, the increase in precision from the vineyard to techniques working with fruit in the cellar has improved.

As a result of the WRE, I can tell over the years that winemakers, their peers, harvest interns, and assistant winemakers' level of conversation and networking are increasing. Especially at the WRE wine tastings, people are more comfortable saying what they taste and think.

Another thing that excites me is mapping the grape ripening curve in Virginia compared to other regions. I have been working on a method for determining grape ripeness as we approach harvest. We are so much riper than we realize since we only look at sugar measured in Brix. I'm still working on a method to quickly and accurately measure in an excellent temporal fashion that is helpful.

We have much interference during harvest, rain, for example, making our sugars come down, so we think we are not ripening, but the vine is still sugar-loading. Another interference is due to heat or some event where the vines stop sugar loading, but we look like we are ripening because the vines are dehydrating.

So, I am trying to develop a user-friendly way to look at how our tannins and anthocyanins are developing and whether they are going up or down. And the berry weight, going up or down, and how much sugar is there per berry. It's going to take me probably three more years. Then I'll have a good tool for the State of Virginia, and we can move away from measuring sugar as the sole ripeness indicator.

What do you like wine lovers to know about you or your wine?

How much thought I put into everything I do. And how much thought goes into Veritas wines? It's not to be ignored. I think about everything, why people are buying our wine, why people are not, what they like, why I like this wine, what our vineyard looks like.

I am overly aware of my surroundings as soon as it's Spring, the vineyard and cellar's look, feel, and smell. I am thoughtful about every barrel I use, every strain of yeast I use, balance, what I will do next, what I can do differently, what I got right, and what I got wrong. There is so much life and so much passion. And so many people share this passion with me, my amazing team.

Which red grapes show promise in the Monticello AVA?

Cabernet Franc, I adore it. When a winemaker finds the right balance of herbal quality with Cabernet Franc's ripeness, that's its best expression. When Cabernet has fresh, graphite, and bell pepper characteristics, it ages out in the bottle like you won't believe; it's so beautiful.

Merlot has been a backbone wine for me, not from a single varietal wine perspective but as a big part of my blending process. And the third grape showing promise is Petit Verdot.

Whites?

Albariño, because everyone I've tasted from Virginia has been good. Petit Manseng, I am working on a style that suits

111

me best—finally, Viognier. My dad has said I have a good hand with Viognier.

I make a style that expresses Virginia Viognier well. Part of it is that I have some of the happiest Viognier in the world. It's planted on the proper slope at the correct aspect. Half the vines were planted in 1999, so the oldest are over twenty. A quarter is in its tenth year, and the other quarter is six years old.

The vineyard sites are different, the older vines get the afternoon sun, and the younger ones get the morning sun. This allows blending fresh, younger, more acidic wine with riper quality wine. I blend it all, keeping them separate until the very end. I also use this Viognier in my Monticello White blend.

Lee Hartman, Head Winemaker at Bluestone Vineyards

Why do you do what you do?

I oversee winemaking and production because of timing and when I came along. My parents weren't building this vineyard as a way for Lee to have a job, but this ended up being the thing I fell in love with. Now my wife, son, and I plan our vacations around the stage of a given vintage.

So, the reason I am doing this is because my parents were doing this. We had a hobby vineyard or garden vineyard of about two-hundred vines. It was a row of Cabernet Sauvignon, next to a row of Cayuga, next to a row of Golden Muscat. and Chardonel. It didn't make complete sense. And about the time I was graduating from college was the time they decided to plant ten-thousand vines.

I aspired to become a tour guide or work in a European museum. I love history, and Europe is the place to be. Although my parents supported me, they asked if I could help plant grape vines until my plans for Europe took root. So, after doing that for a couple of years, I had that very cliché moment where I was looking at a glass of Chardonnay in my hand and said to myself, "Oh, this is just a bunch of dirt and water and sunlight, and I think that's the wildest thing I've ever heard of." From that point, I never looked back.

I have met many fantastic characters along this path, such as the people you interviewed for this book. I made many great friends, and there is no reason, outside all those other people in the industry, that this person who started at twenty-three in the wine industry should be able to do what I am doing. I should not be trusted with hundreds of thousands of dollars worth of fruit every September, except that I can lean on those people, and I have learned so much from talking to them and getting to know them.

So, the rest of the answer is that today one of the main things that keeps me here is the industry I am surrounded by. They are such a vast population that all have this commonality, but being as individual as they can be, it's such a cool thing to be a part of. I love that aspect.

And it's also cool to share what I do with the public; it's something I love. There is no other reason to work one-hundred-hour weeks in September except that you love being a part of this and sharing it with people.

I didn't ask for this, but I can't imagine doing anything else. If a comet stuck Bluestone Vineyard and blew it off the map, this is still what I would do, or we would rebuild it.

What has changed in the Virginia wine industry since you began?

Growth: I have been making wine for fifteen vintages, and many things have changed, but at the same time, the world of wine is slow-moving. It's a big ship with a small rudder. New people come along, and new programs are implemented, but things move slowly.

However, when we opened our doors, we were winery number one hundred ninety-one, then within three to five years, we were approaching three hundred wineries. After that, it clipped along at a snail's pace. I think a lot has changed. When your industry has grown by almost 60% since you opened your doors, that is a lot going on.

We are seeing that Virginia wine might grow again after the pandemic. I'm excited about that growth. The pandemic certainly hampered us. It was a challenging time; even here on the farm, we didn't have concerts for five-hundred people anymore, and specific channels of how we got our wine to people changed.

For the Shenandoah Valley, it has positioned itself to blow up. We are the driest AVA, the largest AVA, and the oldest AVA; we are the most well-defined AVA geographically, from the top of the Blue Ridge Mountains to the top of the Allegany Mountains, and in between is our AVA. And another ingredient is a major highway that runs right through the AVA, providing effortless access to our wineries.

People in the wine industry are coming to understand this. Other Virginia wineries, too, are also understanding this; they are scouting for land, or they've already bought land. It's a great place to grow grapes. And now, a critical mass is growing, and I hope the five existing wineries in Rockingham County grow to five dozen, but we'll see.

Our industry has certainly got a lot smarter. 2010 was my first vintage working with tons and tons of fruit, and I thought, wow, this is easy, and why would anyone make lousy wine? Contrast that with 2011, "the year of the rosé"; it just rained and rained starting in September and didn't stop until Thanksgiving; it was horrible. That was the year I became a winemaker. You learn this is not easy, and you are not in charge of the weather and the elements that get thrown your way; it was a humbling year, especially when there was a tropical storm named Lee that came up the coast.

Fast-forward to 2018, another miserable year; it started raining early and didn't let up. In the Shenandoah Valley in June, we got a foot more rain than usual, and on the other side of the Blue Ridge, they had a foot more than us. Combined, we made better wine in 2018 than in 2011. That is massive growth for the industry; we are more innovative, better connected, and better at giving each other advice. We give either help as neighbors or through organizations like the WRE. Production-wise, we are a much sharper industry than we used to be.

What do you want for Virginia wine?

Essentially, Virginia wine is what it should be and what I want it to be. I don't want it to evolve much more; you can always get better at what you do. Sometimes you will double your efforts to make something 4% better. The folks that get that are already making good, balanced wine.

I want our wine to be available to more people. I want people to get to know and see Virginia wine in the greater context of wine and then appreciate it more.

Not only would I like wine to be the beverage of choice, but if it were, they would realize Virginia makes equally good wine. And for our customers to realize our local region sits between Europe and California, and our wine's taste characteristics are between New and Old-World wine. If people understood Virginia wine better, they would order it more often.

What do you want for the Virginia wine industry?

Continued support for our industry, from tanks to wine presses to yeast, it's good to have the investment and backing from these companies that think what we are doing is worthwhile. And inevitably, during our busiest time, things go wrong, equipment fails, for example, and we need support.

Next would be getting our wine into the marketplace. Production of wine and availability of grapes is not the issue. We need Virginia wine ambassadors throughout the distribution chain who share our vision and know our wine is good to make space for our bottles and attract our attention.

What are you doing now that excites you?

My *Vineyard Site Series*. It's kind of my private-label wines here at Bluestone. It's experimental small lots of wine, nerdy but well-made delicious wines that may not be for everyone. I enjoy making the labels, too; they are scenes from around the vineyard, up-close textural things.

For my Vineyard Site Series, I've made white wine from red grapes called *Odd Bird* and another white from Cabernet Franc called *Orphan No.3*, a collaboration with Hark Vineyards. Then I made a vineyard ferment using Chardonnay, where the juice fermented outside—a rosé Pét-Nat with Chambourcin and an orange skin contact wine with Petit Manseng. And now I'm making a raisin wine called *Desecration Red* with Chambourcin, Cabernet Sauvignon, and Petit Verdot.

This year we are starting sparkling wine production; we now have the equipment in-house and are excited. It is more work for us, but it's rewarding work to make wine by hand.

Also, I am very excited about this year; I'll be opening a wine bar called *Root Stock Wine Bar and Provisions* in downtown Harrisonburg, Virginia. It will be half Bluestone wines, about twenty-five of our wines, and a rotating cast of about the same number of wines from around the world. It will be fun; I'll get to explore the world of wine and have my friends come in and pour their wine. I have a series called *Wine Among Friends*; they come in with several cases of their wine and get to know our customers while we get to know them. We'll continue that at the wine bar.

What do you like wine lovers to know about you or your wine?

I love Chardonnay. We make killer Chardonnay here at Bluestone and around Virginia. Our vineyard's altitude is one thousand four hundred feet; in contrast with Chatham Vineyards in the Virginia Eastern Shore AVA, they are fourteen feet above sea level. And we both make good Chardonnay; they show where they are from so well. So, to me, exploring Chardonnay is exciting; it shows you where it is from and the hand of the winemaker. That is exciting to work with; much balance and stylistic decisions need to go into it. And I love to drink it. Chardonnay is a tough one to beat for me and my money.

I want people to know I am passionate about wine, and I am fortunate to work with it in the capacity I do. Not only this, but I am grateful to be a Virginia and especially a Shenandoah Valley winemaker. Working in the Shenandoah Valley is getting in at the beginning of something that will be big someday.

I am the president of the Shenandoah Valley Wine Growers Association, I see all the work we must do, and I feel fortunate to work with my peers. There is an opportunity for us to stake out a great future here in the Shenandoah Valley and Virginia and to witness this as it happens. I love the winemaking process; it's worth my time and a consumer's time and money to check this stuff out.

What red grapes show promise in Virginia?

The red grapes that show promise here are Cabernet Franc, Merlot, Petit Verdot, and Chambourcin. As for the white grapes, I'd say Vidal Blanc, Petit Manseng, and Chardonnay

The following five sections answer the question, what wine grapes does Virginia have planted? And what is the result of the efforts in terms of accolades awarded by wine professionals?

The sources used as references are the Virginia *Commercial Wine Grape Report* —next, the award-winnings from four wine competitions. The wine competitions are the *Virginia Governor's Cup* representing all of Virginia's AVAs and wine regions. The *Loudoun Wine Awards* cover Loudoun County, Virginia, and part of the Middleburg AVA. The *Monticello Cup Wine Competition* showcases the wines of the Monticello AVA in the Charlottesville, Virginia, area. And the *Shenandoah Cup* wine competition represents the wineries that are members of the Shenandoah Valley Wine Trail and are in the Shenandoah Valley AVA.

Great wine is made in the vineyard; this theme rings true with all the winemakers I know. What better way to gain insight into Virginia's wine industry than to know what is growing in its vineyards and their growth trends?

123

The Commercial Wine Grape Report is generated on behalf of the Virginia Wine Board, with management from the Virginia Vineyards Association and the Virginia Wine Board Marketing Office facilitating data collection.

The annual report contains grape harvest information, a summary of grape production by species, grape variety production, grape production by geographic areas, counties, and year-over-year totals of grape production.

The visuals here were created using data from the 2021 and 2022 reports. The annual Commercial Wine Grape Report is available to the public from *virginiawine.org*.

Tons of Grapes per Year

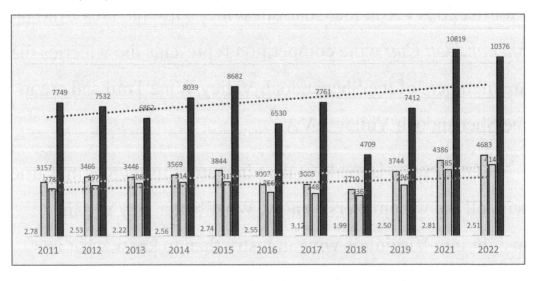

Grape production is depicted in red, trending upwards over time. The 2021 and 2022 vintages have broken out of the norm and are starting what looks like a new and higher trend. The overall average is 7,867 tons of wine grapes per year.

Anecdotal evidence would understand the increase in grape production by the number of new wineries coming online and wineries increasing the acreage of their existing vineyards. The total vineyard acreage is depicted in yellow next to the acreage bearing grapes in green. Given existing space, the immediate potential for more grape production is the difference. The small, leftmost bars are the tons of grapes per acre, trending flat, staying steady at an average of 2.57 tons per acre. As mentioned, 2018's low grape production was due to Virginia's challenging rainy and wet growing conditions.

The potential for growth of the Virginia wine industry seems limitless. Currently, Virginia has 4,683 acres of vineyards across all its regions. By comparison, there are approximately three million acres of farmland in Virginia.

Acres by Grape Type

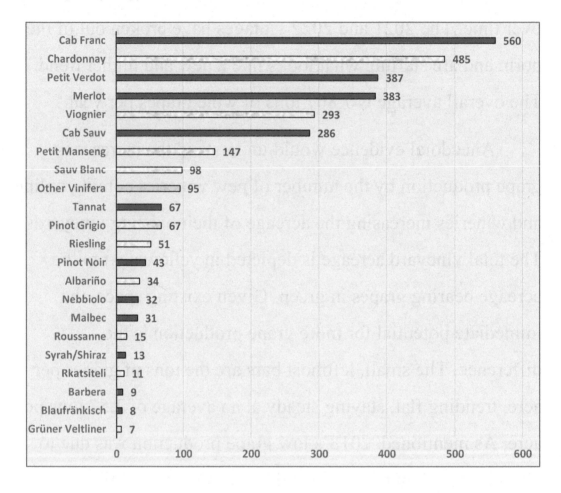

The bulk of the grape species planted throughout Virginia is the world-renowned Vinifera—and Virginia at present favors red Vinifera varieties over whites, 58% to 42%.

Acres of Hybrid and American Grape Types

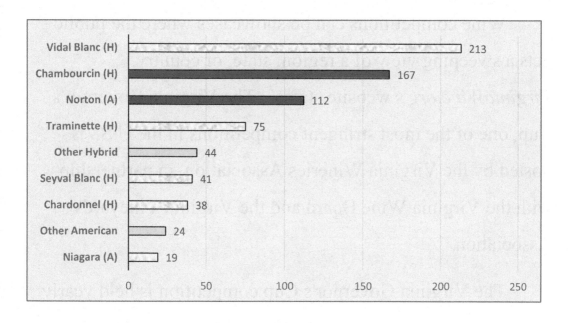

Hybrid grapes are bred to make grape vines or their fruit better. This could mean better suited to a given climate, such as a cold one. Or more resistant to mold, as in a warm climate. Hybrids in Virginia have been successful and welcomed by Virginia wine lovers.

American indigenous grapes, especially Norton, are part of the fabric of success in the Virginia wine industry.

Wine competitions can be showcases where the public gets a sweeping view of a region, state, or country. *VirginiaWine.org*'s website states, "The Virginia Governor's Cup, one of the most stringent competitions in the U.S., is hosted by the Virginia Wineries Association, in partnership with the Virginia Wine Board and the Virginia Vineyards Association."

The Virginia Governor's Cup competition is held yearly, with hundreds of wines awarded bronze, silver, and gold medals. Virginia Governor's Cup results are posted on virginiawine.org, along with winery information and details on winning wines. Not all of Virginia's wineries choose to participate. Some are restricted from participating due to the entrance criteria requiring a certain number of cases to be reserved for sale after the competition.

In addition to the medals awarded, twelve wines are chosen for the Governor's Case from all the gold medal winners, and one wine from the twelve wins the Governor's Cup.

Once the results are in, I love sifting through the medal winners seeing some of my favorite wineries' offerings, comparing my opinions vs. the judges, and discovering new wine and talent from among the Virginia winemakers and wineries.

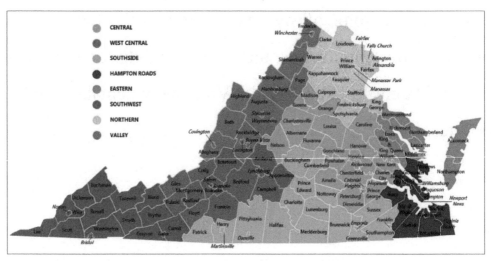

Eight regions of Virginia - University of Virginia Weldon Cooper Center

I analyzed the 2012 to 2023 results of the Governor's Cup available from VirginiaWine.org and have made some interesting observations. For analysis purposes, I used the eight regions of Virginia depicted in the state map above.

The University of Virginia Weldon Cooper Center, Demographics Research Group, provided the map. It can be obtained from their website at *demographics.coopercenter.org/virginia-regions*.

Within these regions lie the AVAs of Virginia; the Monticello AVA is in the Central region; the Middleburg AVA is in the Northern region; and the Shenandoah AVA is in the Valley region.

There are three AVAs in the Eastern and Hampton Roads regions, Northern Neck George Washington Birthplace, Virginia's Eastern Shore, and Virginia Peninsula.

The North fork of Roanoke and Rocky Knob, AVAs, are in the West and Central region. Virginia, North Carolina, and Tennessee share the Appalachian High Country AVA in the Southside region.

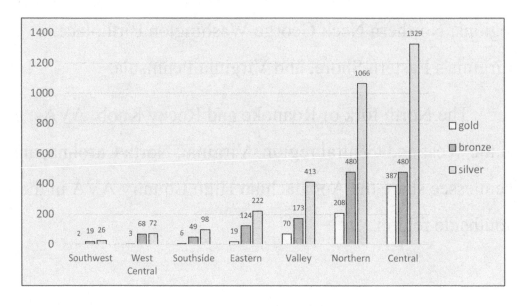

As one of the world's great wine-producing regions, Virginia makes many types and styles of wine made with grapes that fit its soil and climate. Virginia produces high-quality wine in all its regions, with the concentration of winegrowing situated relatively close to the Blue Ridge Mountains in the northwestern and central part of the state.

Vineyards in these areas are planted at higher elevations in well-drained soil, with the positioning of the vines to maximize sun exposure. Most Governor's Cup medal-winning wineries are in the Central, Northern, and Valley regions. Considering the quality of wine produced in these regions, one can understand why American Viticultural Areas were established there.

In the future, it will be advantageous to create more AVAs throughout the state and to establish sub-AVAs within existing AVAs to market and emphasize the uniqueness of terroir, with an eye for preserving land for growing wine.

It is short-sighted to ignore the importance and advantages of creating AVAs designating official places of origin for wine growing, especially when scientific evidence in the form of geologic and climate data demonstrates the uniqueness of a place concerning wine growing. And AVAs allow for marketing, name recognition, and branding of wine and regions.

If necessary large overarching AVAs could first be put in place; then, as in all mature wine regions of the world, subregions can be identified within the larger AVAs.

This model has been successfully demonstrated in California's three-million-acre North Coast AVA. In it sit fifty-four sub-AVAs. These sub-AVAs were created based on their defining climate and soil characteristics.

The world-renowned Napa Valley AVA is a sub-AVA of the North Coast AVA, and the Napa Valley AVA has sixteen sub-AVAs. The sub-AVAs of the Napa Valley AVA were created to focus on more minor, well-understood wine regions' characteristics. This is demonstrated by the Napa Valley sub-AVAs being categorized as valley floor AVAs, mountain AVAs, and the cooler southern AVAs. Each category has characteristics that produce uniqueness in wine, and the AVAs within these categories further define their wine.

A maturing wine region's normal progression is understanding, defining, categorizing, and taking advantage of the place of origin concept. Otherwise, we are left with either winery as places of origin or meaningless blobs as places of origin, as in American Wine or New York Wine. Which begs the question, where in America? And what part of New York?

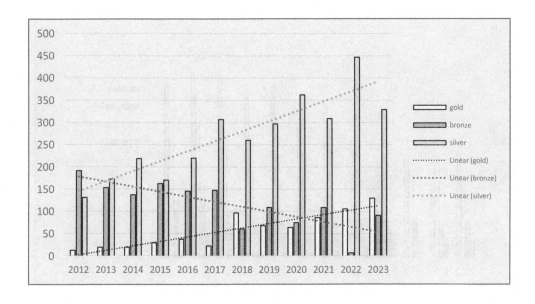

The state trend for gold and silver medals awarded is on a steady rise upward. At the same time, the amount of bronze medal wines has decreased. I interpret this as a reflection of the Virginia wine industry maturing—a wine industry with experienced producers, maturing vineyards, and the positive contribution of ancillary supporting factors. A demanding consumer population and new wineries opening create healthy competition. Also, the contribution of professional resources such as *Virginia Polytechnic Institute, State University,* and the Virginia State government add tremendous value.

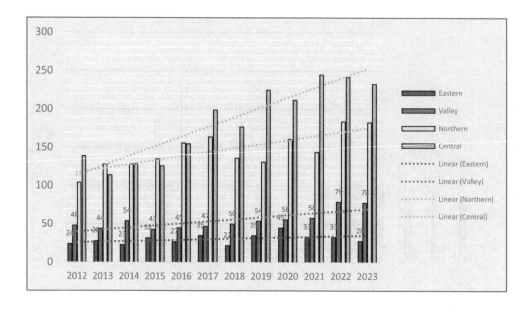

The trend for medals is rising for the four regions shown, Central, Northern, Valley, and Eastern. Over time more wineries are participating, wineries are submitting multiple entries, and more medal-worthy wine is being made. This positive trend indicates an overall increase in the quality and quantity of wine produced across Virginia.

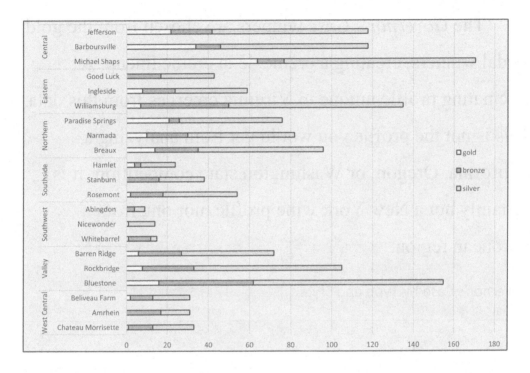

The regional chart on the previous page could be seen as the forest view, while this chart is the forest view with the tallest trees called out. Here we have the top three Governor's Cup medal-winning wineries from each region throughout Virginia.

These wineries are well-known throughout Virginia and are leaders in quality wine production and hospitality. Knowing you are always close to award-winning wine is helpful when visiting Virginia's countryside.

The *Governor's Case* winners are chosen from the gold medal winners, creating a crème de la crème lineup. A fascinating profile unique to Virginia emerges from this data. This is not the profile you would get from analyzing a California, Oregon, or Washington state competition. It is certainly not a New York wine profile, nor one from a European region.

Governor's Case by Type and Style

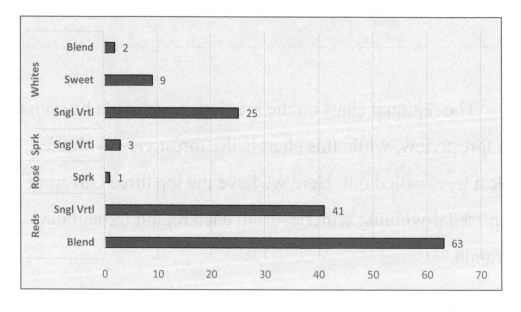

My first observation is that red wine dominates the Governor's Case wines; overall, red blends are the most prominent. However, it is interesting that combined single-varietal red and white wine is greater than red blends.

The next observation is that the array of styles produced is impressive: red blends, white blends; single-varietal reds and whites, dessert wines; sparkling reds; and sparkling rosés. This indicates the maturing Virginia wine industry. When looking in more detail at renowned wine regions of the world, you find the same; in addition to having signature wine, they produce many different styles of wine.

Four of the five types of wine, red, white, rosé, sparkling, and fortified, are represented in the results. Fortified wine is not yet represented, but we can hope. Port is an excellent example of fortified wine; the wine-making process combines brandy (distilled wine) and dry wine, making high-alcohol or fortified wine.

Governor's Case Reds vs. Whites

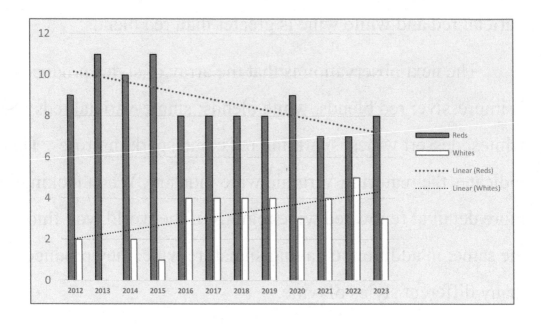

Three times as many red wines have been selected for the Governor's Case since 2012. However, the trend for white wine medals is rising while the number of red wines, in the Governor's case, is declining.

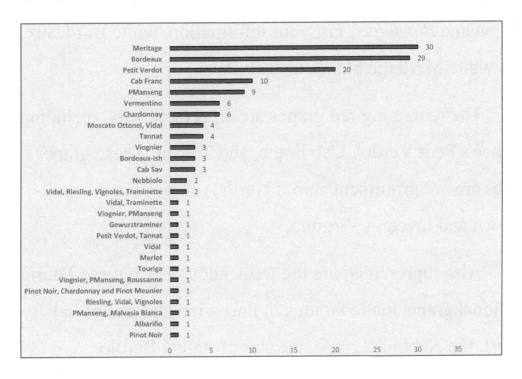

The Governor's Case results showed that red blends are significant contributors. These are either Bordeaux or Meritage blends. Red Bordeaux blends comprise at least two of these grapes, Cabernet Sauvignon, Merlot, Cabernet Franc, Malbec, Petit Verdot, and Carménère. In practice, the world over, Cabernet Sauvignon or Merlot are the leading grapes used.

Meritage wines are also Bordeaux blends, and member wineries of The Meritage Alliance (*meritagealliance.com*) can label and market their flagship wine as a Meritage. The

Meritage concept was created to respect and protect the placename *Bordeaux*. For your information, white Bordeaux and white Meritage blends also exist.

The remaining red grapes are an eclectic mix, including France's Petit Verdot, Cab Franc, and Tannat. These grape types are not prominent across North America but are well-known and loved in Virginia.

Also represented are the tremendous Portuguese Touriga National grape, made famous in Port wine and one of Italy's finest, the Nebbiolo grape, the star of Italian Barolo, Barbaresco, and Gattinara wine.

The Governor's Case whites exhibit a colorful and delicious profile of grapes with Petit Manseng, Vermentino, Viognier, and the ever-present-everywhere Chardonnay leading the way as single varietal wines.

Petit Manseng is widely planted in Southwest France, Vermentino in Sardinia, Italy, and Viognier originates from the Northern Rhône Valley in France.

The white blends are a beautiful collection of the world's best grapes with high acidity and fruit sugar, perfect for sweet dessert wine. The collection includes the proven French hybrids Vidal Blanc, Vignoles, and Traminette, a cross of Gewurztraminer, and a French hybrid. These grapes produce flavorful sweet wine, including Canada's ice wine.

Moscato Ottonel and Riesling grapes hail from the colder regions of Europe, and Malvasia Bianca is the most widely planted Malvasia grape in Italy and has Greek origins.

What is a wine region without sparkling wine? The Governor's Case winners include a single varietal, Blanc de Blanc (sparkling wine from one white grape, usually Chardonnay), a Champagne blend, and a sparkling rosé.

Governor's Case Grape Origins 2012-2023

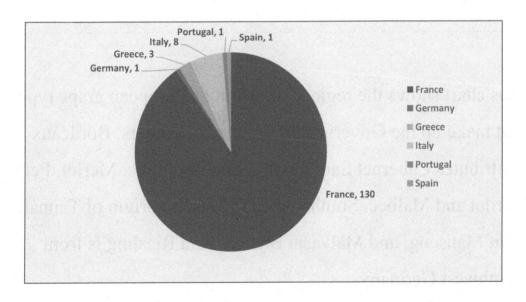

The above chart represents the countries of origin of the grape types that make up the Governor's Case winners and the number of times the grapes appear in the results. Grapes from all the major wine-producing countries are represented, with the bulk coming from France and, to a lesser degree, Italy.

Regions and Country of Origin of Grapes

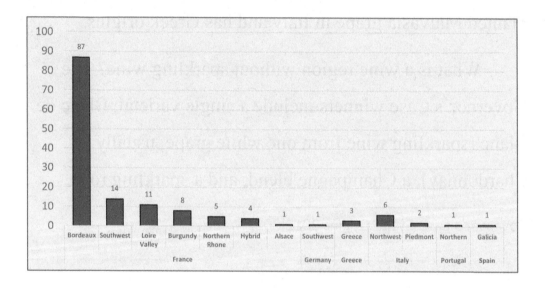

This chart shows the regions of origin of European grape types that make up the Governor's Case medal winners. Bordeaux contributes Cabernet Sauvignon, Cabernet Franc, Merlot, Petit Verdot and Malbec. Southwest France is the origin of Tannat, Petit Manseng, and Malvasia Bianca. And Riesling is from Southwest Germany.

The Loire Valley takes credit for single varietal Cabernet Franc—Burgundy for Chardonnay and Northwest Italy for Vermentino.

The Northern Rhone Valley is the home of our loved Viognier, and Seyval Blanc hails from France. Greece is home to Moscato Ottonel and Vidal Blanc, while Italy's Piedmont gives us Nebbiolo. Northern Portugal contributes Touriga National, the famous Port wine grape. And from Alsace, France, we get Gewurztraminer, while from Galicia, Spain, comes Albariño.

I analyzed publicly available data from the Loudoun Wine Awards website, including 2018 through 2022. The analysis reveals trends and regional profiles and highlights the stars of Loudoun County wine.

To note, the level of effort put into judging large numbers of wines, the planning, logistics, management, and communication of this effort is itself to be awarded gold medals.

The Loudoun Wine Awards website states, "Loudoun County, Virginia, is home to one of the global most exciting emerging wine regions. With nationally and internationally acclaimed wines being produced around the county, this program, presented by the Loudoun Wineries Association, showcases the region's best wines.

The Loudoun Wine Awards judging system utilizes wine industry expert palates, including wine writers, restaurant wine directors, and sommeliers. This will result in a well-rounded selection of top-quality wines endorsed by wine professionals and loved by wine consumers. The annual awards dinner is the highlight of our year. We celebrate the award-winning wines from the competition, and the Winemaker, Winegrower, and Wine Ambassador of the Year."

As a disclaimer, I do not have a complete set of data. For example, if they exist, the bronze medal winners or the number of wines not receiving medals. This limits but does not prevent analysis and valuable findings.

According to the data analyzed from 2018 to 2022, thirty-four wineries have been awarded five-hundred and ten awards. Eighty-three gold medals, three-hundred fifty-three silver medals, fifty-seven Best of Class awards, and seventeen special awards.

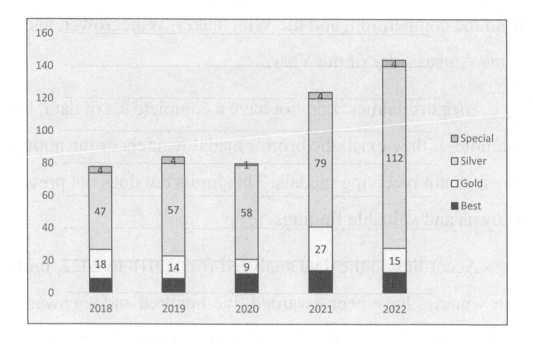

The special awards include accolades for winemakers, winegrowers, and wine ambassadors and a Chairman's Grand Awards category for outstanding wines. The data shows that the number of wines evaluated and awards given are trending upwards; from 2018 to 2022, the number of awards almost doubled.

Wineries Receiving Awards

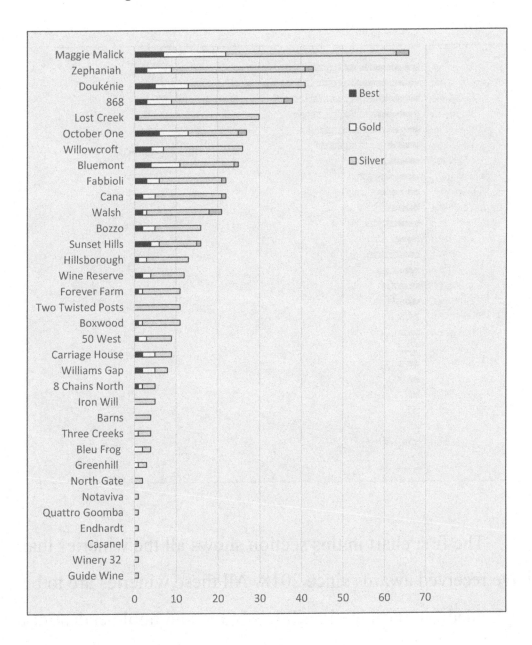

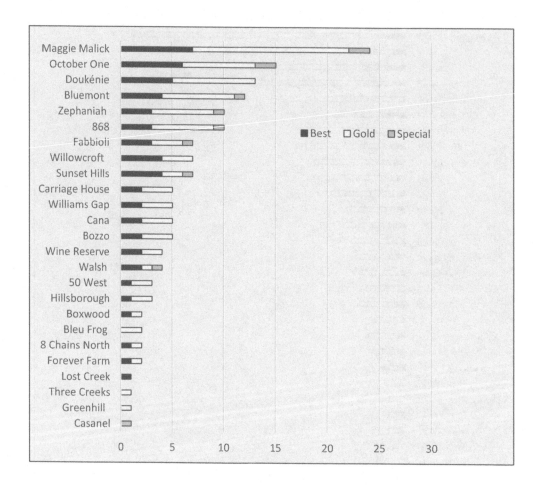

The first chart in this section shows all the wineries that have received awards since 2018. All these wineries are to be applauded for participating. It is a brave and noble endeavor to have your work product examined, evaluated, compared, and put on display. And competition allows wine producers to see their wine through the objective eyes of experts. Competition also has a way of exerting pressure on the industry to increase the quality of its products.

The second chart is a closer look at the most award-winning wineries. I have removed the silver medals awards from this chart to zoom in on the set of high performers.

Interestingly the top four wineries are located on a line running north-to-southwest, east of the Shenandoah River, on the eastern side of the Blue Ridge Mountains, and not far from the Ashby Gap. The Ashby Gap is an air gap in the Blue Ridge Mountains on the border of Clarke County, Fauquier County, and Loudoun County in Virginia. The Appalachian trail passes through the gap, north to south, while U.S. Route 50 passes through the Ashby gap from east to west.

Evaluation of Loudoun County shows a distinct topography, and soil runs north to south along the foothills of the Shenandoah. This could be called the Northern Piedmont of Virginia; piedmont, translated from Italian, is the foot of the mountains or foothills. In this case, the foothills of the Blue Ridge Mountains

Here are the thirty grape types that have received awards. This data reinforces what we already know about Loudoun County wine by experience; Cabernet Franc is the prince of Northern Virginia wine.

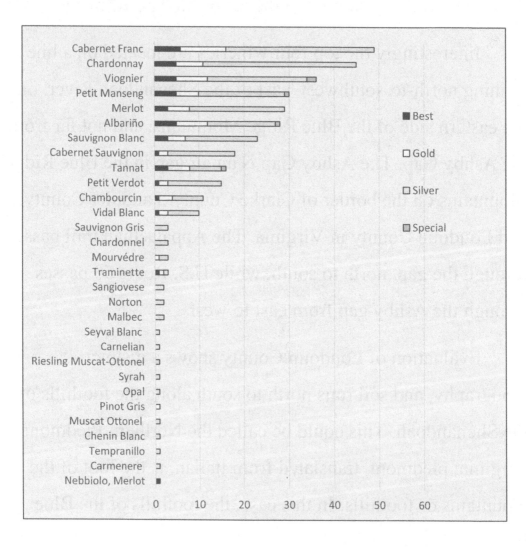

Merlot is just a little behind and planted along the northern Piedmont at higher elevations, creating rich, smooth, and expressive wines. Based on my experience Merlot is poised to be a signature wine of Loudoun County.

Meanwhile, white wine grapes such as Viognier, Chardonnay, Albariño, Petit Manseng, and Sauvignon Blanc thrive in Loudoun County. Albariño and Petit Manseng are gaining notoriety more recently and show promise of being stars of this region.

Best of Class, Gold, Chairmans Grand Awards

Here are all the grape types that comprise the recipients of Gold, Best of Class, and Chairmans Grand Awards. These wines might be called the best of the best wines.

Interesting to note that whites make up five of the top ten wines. Other interesting points are how well Tannat did and how many times it appears as a single varietal wine or in a blend.

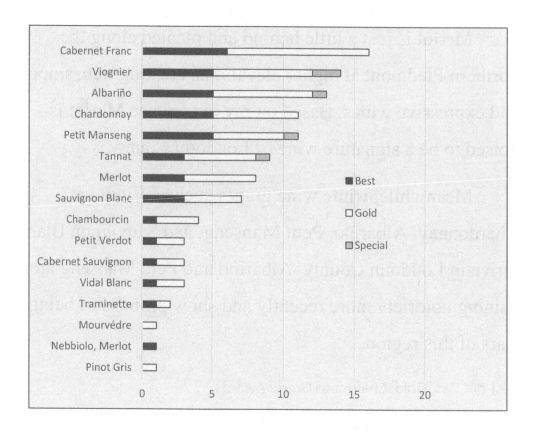

The presence of Nebbiolo and Pinot Gris/Grigio stirs one's interest and hope for further investment in these famous grape types. These grape types produce outstanding wine in Italy's northern parts. Nebbiolo in The Piedmont and Pinot Gris/Grigio in Trentino-Alto Adige.

154

From 2018 to 2022, the ratio of all the award-winning wines by type shows that more white wines are winning than red. By contrast, at the state level, the percentage of award-winning wine shows red wine out winning white by 3 to 1.

This has not always been the case. The chart below shows that in Loudoun County, white wine awards have steadily increased while red wines receiving awards are trending downward.

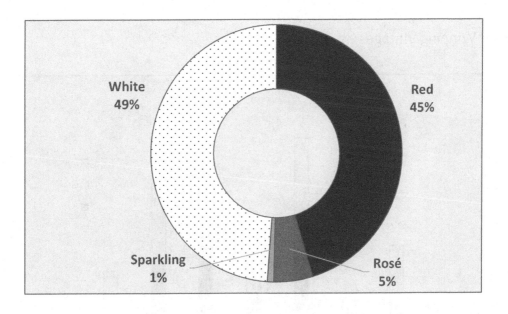

Award Winning Trends, Red vs. White Wines

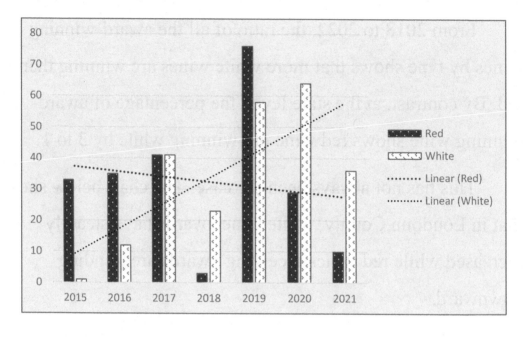

Award Winning Vintages

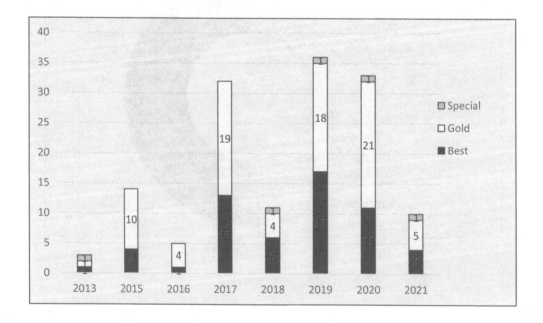

Looking at awards by vintage year with the silver awards removed highlights four outstanding recent years, 2015, 2017, 2019, and 2020. Experientially I can attest to the fact that these are good vintages. With the reds released, I find richness, depth of flavor, medium acidity, and smooth, ripe tannin structure. The whites from these vintages are vibrant, with nice acidity, and rich in flavors with a balanced structure.

Findings from good and challenging years

Informative findings can be observed from good and challenging wine-growing years. The two charts below show that in Loudoun County, weather conditions vary from year to year enough so that their impact is detected in the award data.

For example, the first chart represents red wine and demonstrates a noticeable void in award-winning red wine in 2018. This is a direct correlation to challenging wine-growing weather conditions. Each line of the below charts represents a grape type, and the rise and fall across vintage years is the accumulative number of awards. This data also validates the expertise of the wine judges that did not award inferior wines from a difficult growing season.

Red Wine Awards by Vintages and Grape Type

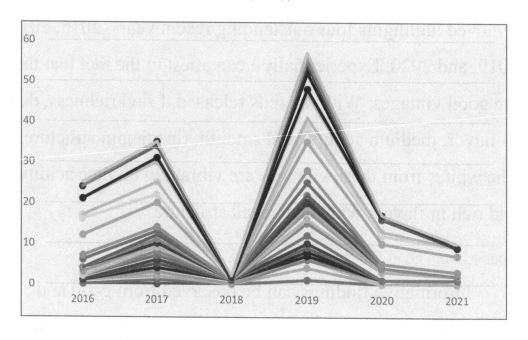

White Wine by Vintages and Grape Type

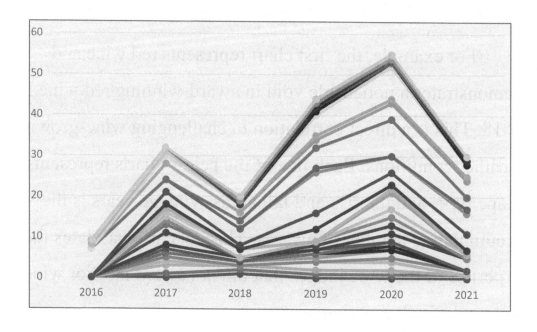

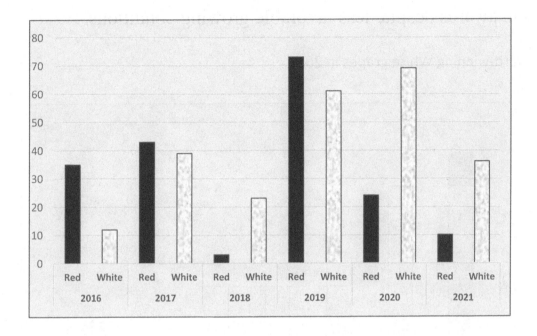

Also, the data shows that climate conditions can favor red wine one year and white the next. 2017 and 2019 seem to be as close to balanced years for red and white wine awards as possible. Two thousand sixteen favors reds, while 2018, 2020, and 2021 favor white wine over reds for award reception.

In Loudoun County, 2018 was a challenging year for winegrowing. It rained off and on throughout the entire growing season. Some wineries did not bottle red wine, and others chose to make rosés, but all was not lost; many white wines were still available and winning awards.

This chart shows which grapes produced white wine that won awards despite less favorable growing conditions.

Award-winning White grapes in 2018

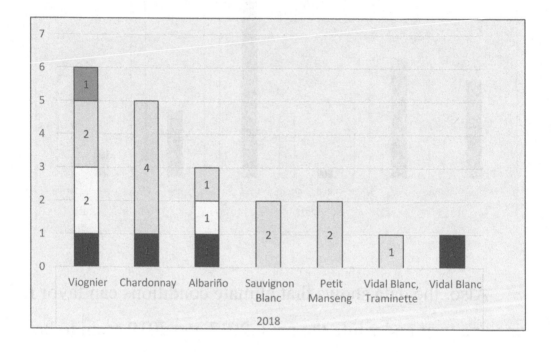

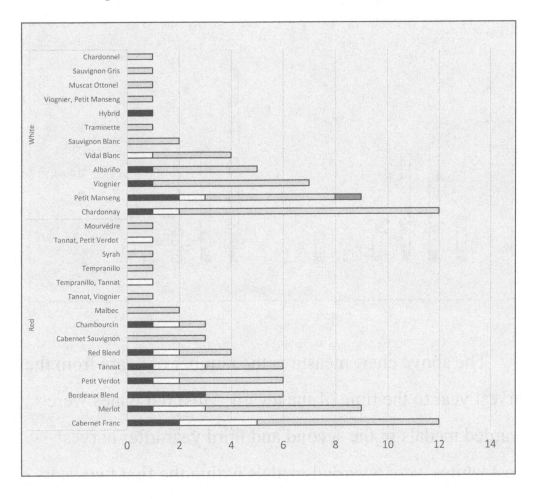

Twenty-nineteen is the most balanced vintage for Loudoun County wine awards. There were close to equal awards for red and white wine. And the number of awards is the largest overall with the data analyzed. The above chart represents red and white grapes that won awards in twenty nineteen.

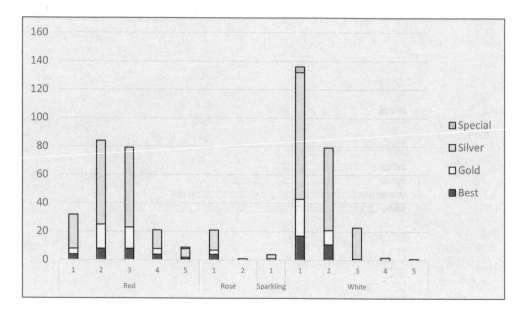

The above chart measures the number of years from the harvest year to the time of the award. Most red wines were awarded medals in the second and third year after harvest. Most whites were awarded medals within the first two years of harvest.

For sparkling and rosés, awards were given within a year of harvest. Also, note that there are sweet spots for releasing with each type. Red wines show well in the second and third year after harvest, dramatically declining in the fourth and subsequent years.

Monticello Cup Wine Competition

Monticello Cup Wine Competition has been held for more than thirty years. The friendly competition among member wineries celebrates the best wines of the Monticello AVA. To be entered, at least 85% of a wine must be made from fruit in the Monticello AVA and be produced by a member of the Monticello Wine Trail.

Awards and Medals by Year 2015-2023

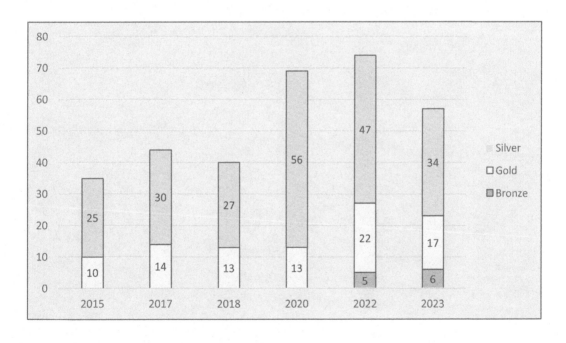

Thanks to the Monticello Wine Trail for providing the award data for my analysis (*monticellowinetrail.com*). The data spans the competitions from 2015 to 2023, excluding 2016 and

2021. Meaningful observations can be made from the thirty-eight wineries' submissions of three-hundred thirty-two wines spanning sixteen vintages.

The data shows that the number of wines evaluated, and awards given are trending upwards; from 2015 to 2022, the number of awards almost doubled.

Wineries Receiving Awards from 2015-2023

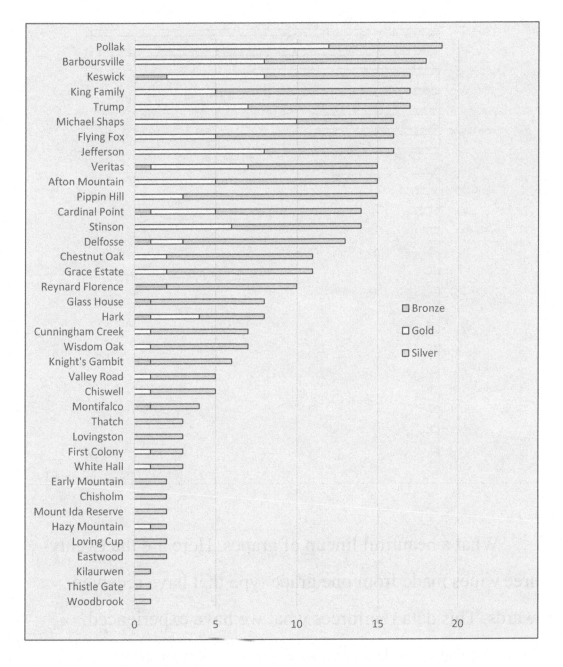

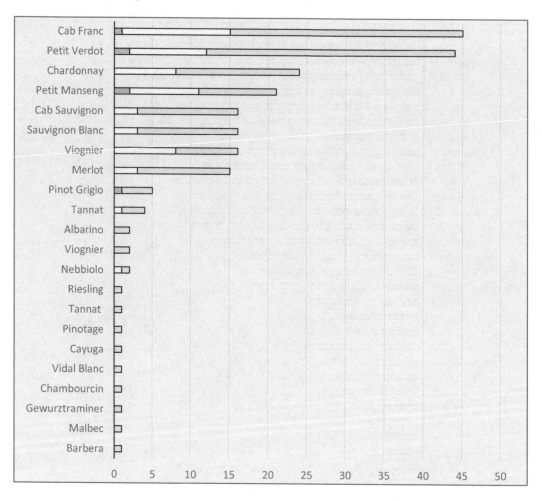

What a beautiful lineup of grapes. Here are the twenty-three wines made from one grape type that have received awards. This data reinforces what we have experienced: Cabernet Franc makes delicious wine in Virginia.

In the Monticello AVA, Petit Verdot may as well be tied to Cab Franc. This grape is a rising star in Virginia wine, making noteworthy, significant, tannic, and ageable wines.

Cabernet Sauvignon is a late-ripening grape and does well in the warm Central Virginia climate. Merlot, another promising grape in Virginia, equals Cabernet Sauvignon in awards. Meanwhile, white wine grapes like Chardonnay, Petit Manseng, Viognier, and Sauvignon Blanc thrive in the Monticello AVA.

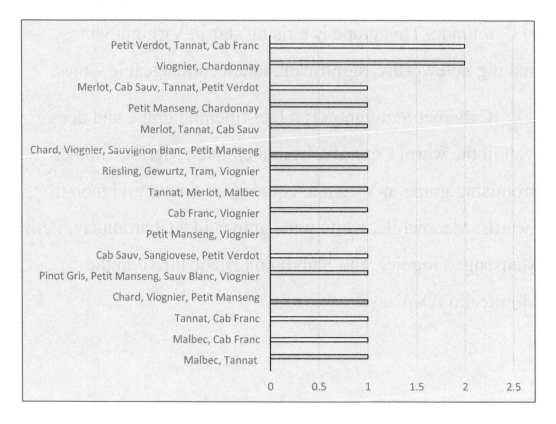

Tannat, Viognier, Petit Manseng, and Cabernet Franc appear most frequently in these blends. Tannat adds a tannic structure to the wine, while Viognier adds body and floral aromas. Petit Manseng contributes acid, or backbone, to wine, and Cabernet Franc adds elegance and gives a peppery fragrance.

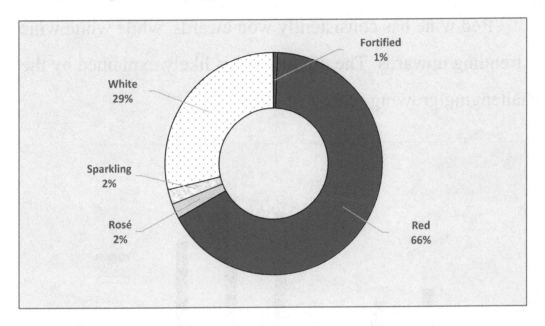

Red wine awards outpace whites by a large margin in the Monticello AVA. Sparkling and rosé wine make a small showing, and fortified wine is an exciting and welcome award winner. The Monticello AVA is to be recognized for producing award-winning wines in all five types; red, white, rosé, sparkling, and fortified.

Fortified wines are a blend of wine and brandy, which is a wine that has gone through the distillation process. These blends have high alcohol levels for wine, as in the high teens to 20% ABV.

Red wine has consistently won awards, while white wine is trending upwards. The dip in 2019 is likely explained by the challenging growing season of 2018.

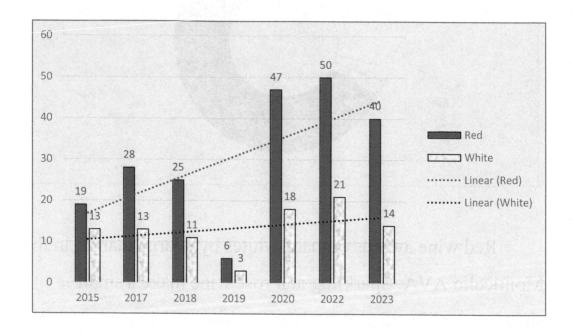

Twenty-seventeen is by far the most awarded vintage of the years I analyzed. This and twenty-nineteen are also well-balanced vintages red vs. white wine awards. This is true in the Monticello AVA and across the State of Virginia.

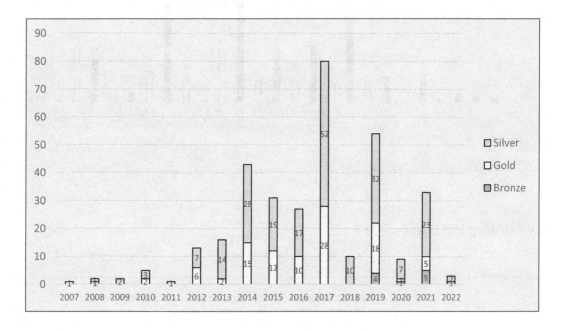

Red vs. White Wine Awards by Vintages

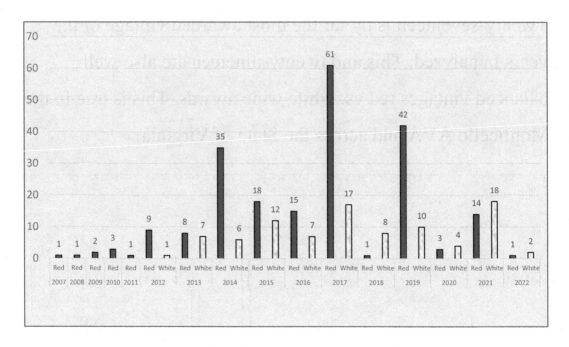

Award-Winning Grapes 2017

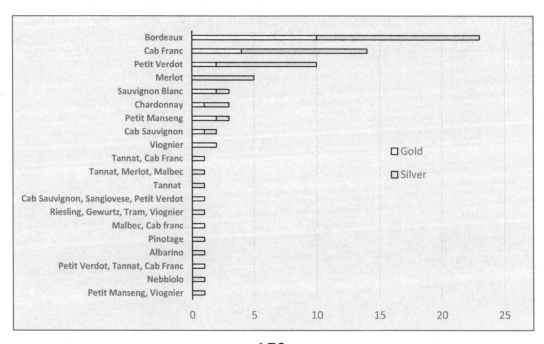

Shenandoah Cup Wine Competition

The Shenandoah Valley Wine Trail holds the annual Shenandoah Cup wine competition. The first competition was held in 2019 to showcase the Shenandoah Valley AVA's fine wine and excellent growing conditions. Wine submitted for judging must be at least 75% Shenandoah Valley AVA wine and produced by a member of the Shenandoah Wine Trail (*shenandoahvalleywinetrail.com*)

Medal-Winning Wine Types

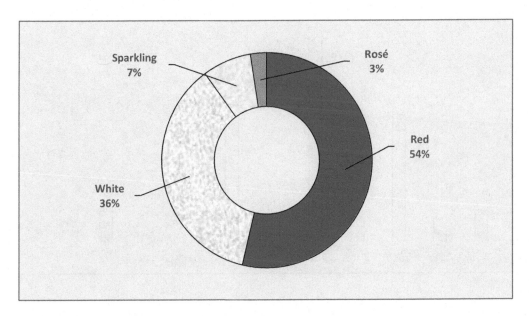

Red wine is represented more in the award-winnings than in some other Virginia regions. Understandably, reds would be prominently embodied, given the favorable growing conditions in the Shenandoah AVA, with long growing seasons, comparatively less rainfall than east of the Blue Ridge Mountains, and a healthy diurnal shift in temperature day to night.

Sparkling wine makes up 7% of the awards given; this is a promising piece of data. And rosé wine being represented is a delight; I view this as a sign of a maturing wine region.

Medal Winning Vintages

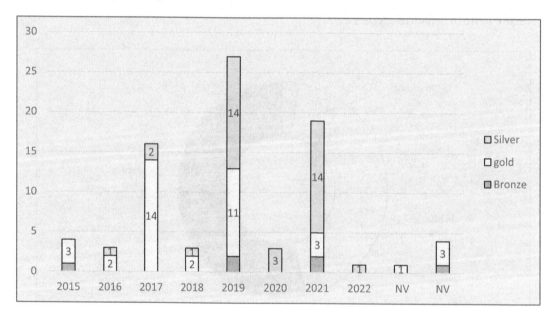

Award-winning vintages emerge from the data and can be attested to from anecdotal evidence. The 2017 and 2019 vintages were stellar years for the Shenandoah Valley AVA.

Medal Winning Wineries

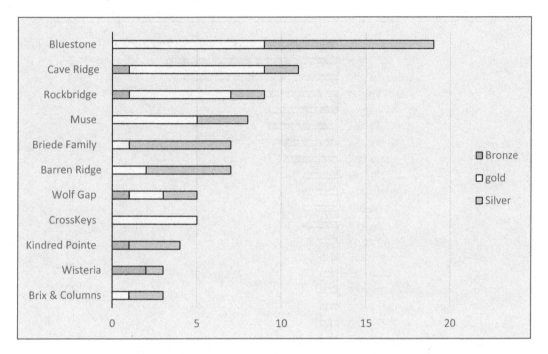

Medal-winning wineries exist throughout the Shenandoah Valley, making this region a star in Virginia. As more wineries come into existence, existing wineries grow, and the Shenandoah Cup wine competition, which started in 2019, becomes more popular, more data will be available for analysis.

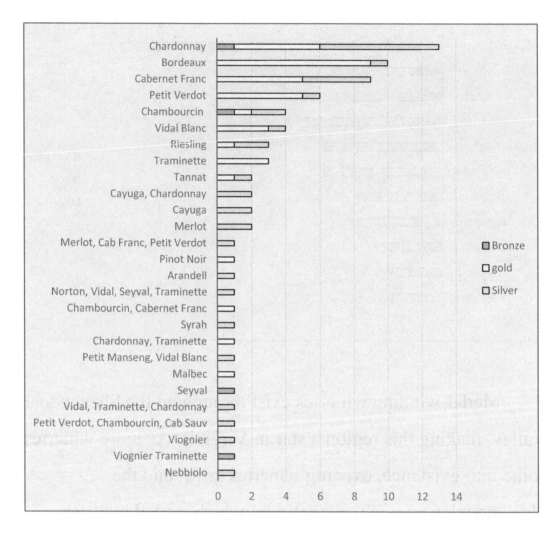

What a fantastic lineup of grape types winning awards in the Shenandoah Valley AVA. The representation of hybrids as single-varietal wines is exciting, and their successful use as blending grapes is apparent.

Hybrids represent three out of the top ten wines winning medals; they are Chambourcin, Vidal Blanc, and Traminette. The representation of Traminette as a blending grape is unique. This grape adds floral and spicy characteristics to wine. The German word for adding spice is würzt, and one of the parent grapes of Traminette is Ge*würzt*raminer, itself a spicy-flavored grape.

Red Bordeaux blends and single varietal Petit Verdot, Cabernet Franc, and Tannat are well represented in the top ten medal winners.

Chardonnay produces unique site-specific Chardonnay wine in the Shenandoah Valley, and I hope that it leads the way to encourage the region and state to produce more.

Virginia State Wine Organizations

Virginia Vineyards Association

The Virginia Vineyards Association (*virginiavineyardsassociation.org*) began in 1979 as a joint effort among Virginia viticulturists, wineries, and Virginia Polytechnic Institute and State University to oversee and promote the following areas of mutual interest. The viticultural interests of Virginia; growth of commercial grape growing as a significant component of Virginia agriculture; cultivation of all species of grapes; public recognition of products made from Virginia grapes; establishment and maintenance of mutually beneficial relationships with local, state, and federal government agencies; free exchange of information and ideas with professional and amateur enthusiasts.

The Virginia Wine Board

Created by the Virginia General Assembly in 1984 as part of Virginia's Department of Agriculture and Consumer Services, the Virginia Wine Board promotes the interests of vineyards and wineries in the Commonwealth through research, education, and marketing. The Virginia Wine Board funds the Virginia Wine Board Marketing Office.

The Board fulfills the following duties. The Virginia Wine Promotion Fund receives funding and dispenses it for wine-related projects and initiatives. Contracts research to improve viticultural and enological practices in the Virginia wine industry. Promotes education about and appreciation for Virginia wines. Promotes the growing of wine grapes and wine production throughout the Commonwealth. Disseminates information on wine and viticultural topics. Contracts marketing, advertising, and other programs that promote the growth of the state's wine industry and the enjoyment of Virginia wines. Collaborates with state, regional, national, and international organizations on their work related to Virginia's wine industry.

Virginia Winery Distribution Company

Established in 2008, the Virginia Winery Distribution Company (VWDC), vwdc.org, is a non-profit, non-stock corporation created by the Virginia Department of Agriculture and Consumer Services (VDACS) to provide wholesale wine distribution services for Virginia farm wineries. Many wineries in the Commonwealth use VWDC to distribute their wines to local retailers.

Formed in 1983, the Virginia Wineries Association (VWA) grew out of the desire of owners of Virginia wineries to create a wine community that shared ideas and resources to benefit everyone in the Virginia wine industry. As a non-profit trade organization, the VWA advocates for the industry in several areas.

The VWA promotes viticulture and vintner practices that ensure the highest quality wine production among its member wineries.

Education about Virginia wines and appreciation for their distinctive qualities among consumers are ongoing initiatives of the VWA.

As a trade organization, the VWA helps develop increased market share for Virginia wines.

The VWA supports continued research into the relationship between wine and health.

A thriving wine industry is growing, so the VWA favors the industry's continued expansion statewide.

Regional Wine Organizations

Loudoun Wineries & Winegrowers Association

The Loudoun Wineries and Winegrowers Association (LWWA), *loudounwine.org* enables the success of the Loudoun County wine industry by promoting agriculture and social stewardship and by facilitating marketing, legislation, education, and communications between members wineries, winegrowers, and their partners.

Wine Professionals Association

The Wine Professionals Association (*novawpa.org* or *cvillewpa.org*) exists to promote, support, and improve the Virginia wine industry by connecting consumers to the local wine industry, our member-professionals to the local wine industry, and local members to local members.

It comprises certified wine professionals, aspiring wine professionals, supporters, and businesses. We are a nonprofit, member-based, regional association – 501c (6).

We connect consumers to local wine by promoting wine businesses via advertising, education, events, and online content. We connect our member professionals to the local wine industry through staffing, access to association members for business opportunities, and acting as an information exchange center, ex: wine industry trends. We perform business consulting: modeling, idea creation, growth strategies, validation of projects, marketing, and partnerships. Improving process and quality control, internal collaboration, and communication. We mentor aspiring wine professionals, provide educational assistance through financial grants, and lobby the state of Virginia on behalf of the wine industry. We connect local members to local members through association events, member events, mentoring fellow members, and participating in association projects and meetings.

Winemakers Research Exchange

The Winemakers Research Exchange (WRE) was established officially in 2014 by a small group of innovating winemakers in the Monticello AVA, with funding from the Monticello Wine Trail to improve ways to make distinctive, quality wine on the East Coast of the U.S.

The chosen method of operation is through practical, production-scale experimentation to test the application of techniques, products, and approaches in Virginia wineries on Virginia fruit. The WRE maintains an online presence via a Facebook group (*www.facebook.com/vawrex*) and its website, *winemakersresearchexchange.com*.

The Shenandoah Valley Wine Growers Association

A nonprofit regional trade association with an active membership of Shenandoah Valley wineries, businesses, and folks interested in wine. The Association's vision is to lead in the promotion and protection of Shenandoah Valley AVA as one of the finest winegrowing regions in the world; to enhance the future of Shenandoah Valley through the preservation and enhancement of its resources: its land, wines, and people; create a unified voice to advocate the common interests of our members; and to meet the challenges of our dynamic, global industry with innovation and integrity.

Wine Festivals

Virginia Wine Expo

Lonely Planet named Richmond's Top Ten Must-visit list of the US destinations you need to see. If there is one event in Richmond that encapsulates the excellent craft beverage and food scene in Virginia, it is the Virginia Wine Expo.

Taste of Monticello Wine Trail Festival

Wine Enthusiast magazine recently dubbed the Charlottesville area one of the world's top wine destinations. The festival celebrates and embodies the area's affinity for great wine, with over thirty wineries in the beautiful Blue Ridge Mountain area. The wine festival includes special winemaker events and the Monticello Cup Awards celebration. It culminates with a massive wine tasting where attendees can sample various local wines from wineries.

Virginia Wine Festival

The annual Virginia Wine Festival is held in October at upscale One Loudoun in Ashburn, Virginia. You can taste Virginia wines and ciders, sample local cuisine, and purchase wine by bottle and case.

The annual festival includes wine tastings from throughout the Shenandoah AVA, music, craft vendors, and food trucks on the grounds of the beautiful Museum of the Shenandoah Valley to celebrate the wines and culture of the Shenandoah Valley.

Acid: Naturally occurring grape acids taste fresh, like orange juice or a tart apple.

Aerated Sparkling Wine: A term found on wine labels for sparkling wine with injected CO_2 to create bubbles, as in carbonated soft drinks.

Aeration: Exposing wine to oxygen by swirling it in a glass or pouring it into another vessel.

Appellation: A defined and understood geographic area designated for producing wine.

Aroma: unique smells associated with a grape variety, for example.

Blanc de Blanc: White wine from white grapes.

Body/full body: How heavy or thick wine feels in the mouth.

Botrytis: Botrytis cinerea, or noble rot, is a grape fungus that concentrates a grape's juice.

Bouquet: The collection of all aromas after a wine has aged in a bottle.

Brix: A measure of grape sugar at harvest.

Brut: Very dry Champagne with no detectable sweetness.

Chewy: a description of wine that seems almost chewable, dense, or sticky.

Complex: A wine with pleasing aromas and flavors that develop as you drink.

Dark/black fruit: Aromas and flavors in wine resembling dark-colored fruit, ex: plums, blackberries, and black cherries.

Decant: Pouring wine out of the bottle and leaving the sediment behind.

Demi-sec: A sweet Champagne or sparkling wine.

Dry wine: A wine with no detectable sweetness, 0.2% or less sugar.

Earthy: Aromas found in wine, like the smells of soil, mushrooms, leaves, and the forest.

Estate bottled: Wine from an estate that does everything from growing to bottling.

Fault: A defect with wine, usually detected by bad, odd, off-putting smells and tastes.

Finish: The taste and feel of wine once swallowed. Long-lasting flavors are considered better.

Fortified wine: Wine blended with brandy containing between 16% and 20% alcohol by volume.

Hot: Wine where alcohol is detected over other flavors and aromas.

Lees: Yeast after fermentation; sur lie is a French term meaning the wine is left in contact with yeast cells to improve the wine's flavor and texture.

Legs: streaks of wine running down the inside of a glass, also called tears or church windows.

Meritage: since Bordeaux is a protected placename, this invented word is used for marketing Bordeaux blends. Usually, the grapes used are Cabernet Sauvignon, Merlot, and Cabernet Franc. The Meritage Alliance organization created this term, and criteria apply when using it on labels; an example is that the Meritage Alliance strongly recommends that wineries label only their best blend as a Meritage.

New World: this term is used to express wine not from Europe with a prominent fruitiness.

Nose: The smell of wine.

Oxidation: A substance reacts when oxygen combines with its molecules, as when steel rusts when exposed to air.

Pétillant: Lightly sparkling.

PetNat: an abbreviation for naturally petillant (bubbly) wine that is slightly sweet, gently fizzy, and has low alcohol.

Red fruit: Aromas and flavors in wine resembling red-colored fruit, ex: cherries, cranberries, strawberries.

Reserve: better or best wine from a producer; this is a regulated word in some U.S. states and Europe.

Residual sugar: Grape sugar left after fermentation in semi-sweet and sweet wine.

Single varietal: Wine from one grape type.

Smoky: The aroma or flavor of smoke in wine occurs naturally caused by barrel aging.

Sulfites: Naturally occurring and added to wine to help preserve it.

Tannin: A plant compound that tastes a little bitter and can cause a drying sensation in the mouth.

Terroir: All aspects affecting wine, the climate, location, soil, and winemaking practices.

Vintage year: Wine released on a year of good production.

Vintage: wine produced from a specific year's grapes, as in a 2020 vintage.

Winegrowing: All aspects of wine production from the vineyard to the bottle.